GAME
of my LIFE

PHILLIES

BOB GORDON

SportsPublishingLLC.com

ISBN 13: 978-1-59670-257-8

Publishers: Peter L. Bannon and Joseph J. Bannon Sr.
Senior managing editor: Susan M. Moyer
Art director: Dustin J. Hubbart

Sports Publishing L.L.C.
804 North Neil Street
Champaign, IL 61820
Phone: 1-877-424-2665
Fax: 217-363-2073
SportsPublishingLLC.com

Printed in the United States of America

CIP data available upon request.

CONTENTS

CHAPTER 1

BOB WINE

"I'm coming up on 50 years in baseball," says Bob Wine. "It's really tough to pick the one game I'd call the game of my life. Let's see, there was the first game I ever played up here. I hit a line drive to right field and Roberto Clemente came in and slid and made a great catch. I guess I realized I was playing in the big leagues at that point. I had driven down here from Buffalo that same day. It took an all-day drive to make it to the game in time. It was quite a ride. I had never been to Philly before and naturally we got lost en route.

"But let's see, as for other games I remember. . . . We had that good ball club in '64—there were lots of great games and memories that season. Certainly, winning the World Series in '80 when I was a Phillies coach was tremendous. But what game do I think of most? It was the game when my first son was born."

MEET BOB WINE

Robert Paul Wine, Sr. grew up in Long Island. The Phillies scouted him and signed him in 1957.

"I went down to Johnson City, Tennessee," Bob recalls. "Chris Short started there with me. We were the only two guys that eventually made it up to the majors. We roomed in a house with about 12 other guys. I started out sleeping on the porch. There wasn't enough space inside, so the porch became my room. As various guys left the team or got called up, each of the others behind them moved further into the house into a better room. The team gave us 75 cents for meal money each day. We got $1.50 if we had to get a hotel room."

"This all happened at one of those 'Rookie Schools' as they called them back then," he explains about getting beaned in the minors. "It was what you would call an 'Instructional League' today."

Wine made his first appearance in the majors on September 20, 1960. The last-place Philadelphia Phillies lost a twin bill to the World Series-bound Pittsburgh Pirates that day. Facing Harvey Haddix and Clem Labine, Wine went hitless in four at-bats. He spent the following season back in the minors because the Phils already had a good shortstop, Ruben Amaro Sr. However, the New York native was called up to the majors to stay in May, 1962.

"When Ruben (Amaro, Sr.) was activated to military reserve duty, the Phils brought me up," Bob explains. "When Ruben returned to the squad (on July 20), we split the shortstop duty. One of us played shortstop and the other would move over to third base."

"Ruben and I have remained best of friends," Bob emphasizes. "Our wives are best friends. In fact, Ruben and his wife got married the same day as I married my wife—on December 9. After our first son Robby was born, the Amaros had David. Then we had Kenny and the Amaros had Ruben Jr.

"When I got to the Phils, it was a great time in my life. The team wasn't good at that point, but we were starting to show some promise by '62. Then we put up a good winning percentage in '63 and finished in the first division. In those days, practically every professional ballplayer in town lived at the old Walnut Park Plaza—all the Phillies and all the Eagles lived there. The Plaza was the only place that didn't make you sign a year lease. So when ballplayers were forced to leave Philadelphia because of trades and the like, they didn't lose money.

"After I was here a couple of years, we rented Tommy Lasorda's old house. Tommy never did a thing to that place! His brother was in the construction business. He and other relatives did all the work around the house. Tommy never did a thing. He never even cut the lawn. Eventually we ended up buying the place. We've lived here ever since."

Wine played with the Phils until 1969, earning a reputation as a fine fielding shortstop with a cannon arm. That distinction made him

When Bob Wine settled in Philadelphia, he bought Tommy Lasorda's house. He still lives there (Wine, not Lasorda). *Photo by Brace Photography*

the first Phillie ever to win a Gold Glove in 1963. The Phillies put him on the board in the expansion draft and the Montreal Expos plucked him as the 23rd pick overall in the draft. Roberto Pena had taken the shortstop job from him in '68 and Wine wasn't seeing much action with the Phils. With Montreal, he was again thrust into a starting role. He held it for only one season. In his second year in Montreal, Tim Foli won the starting shortstop position. Foli arrived in Montreal via a blockbuster deal that brought him, Ken Singleton, and Mike Jorgensen to the Expos in exchange for Rusty Staub— known in francophone Montreal as *le Grand Orange*. On July 10, 1972, Bob was released by the Expos. He soon found a home in the Phillies coaching ranks where he remained until 1983.

Wine headed to Atlanta in '84. In '85, he and Eddie Haas split duty as the Braves' skipper. In '86, Chuck Tanner became the Braves' manager and Bobby accepted the role of advance scout. He's been fulfilling that role ever since.

SETTING THE STAGE

On June 24, 1962, following a twin-killing over the hapless Houston Colt .45s, the Phils ascended into seventh place in the ten-team National League. There were no divisions at that time. Winning a pennant was still a best-of-162-game thing. Philadelphia would occupy the seventh slot for the next three months, except for a brief two-day dalliance in sixth place.

The nucleus of the squad—the cast that was destined to bring so much excitement and heartache to the Quaker City in '64—was starting to hit its stride. In the first half of the '62 season, the Phils posted a 34–47 record. In the second half, they improved to 47–33. Going into the July 13 contest, the 37–50 Phils were starting to turn things around.

THE GAME OF MY LIFE
JULY 13, 1962
BY BOB WINE

I was starting at shortstop that day and my wife was due. The Phils at that point in the season felt we were a good team but we had not been playing good ball. I think we had lost the night before (ex-

4

Phillie, Jack Sanford beat Jack Hamilton 5–3). We had Dennis Bennett on the mound, and I think Billy O'Dell went for the Giants.

The game was scoreless when I came to bat in the third. Sammy White opened the inning with a single and I followed with a single to right. Bennett bunted and the Giants misplayed it into a single. We made a couple of outs and it looked like the Giants were going to escape with no damage. But Ted Savage and Roy Sievers followed with singles and we put three on the board.

I singled again on my second at-bat in the fourth. Both pitchers started to settle in. The Giants got one run back the next inning, I believe. I came up a few innings later (the seventh) and doubled for my third hit. In the eighth I grounded out with men on base, but we were leading 3–1. The Giants got one run back in the top of the ninth, but Willie Mays grounded into a double play that I started, and their rally fizzled. We won it 3–2. Immediately after the game, I went to the hospital and my son Robbie was born. You know, Robbie made it to the majors too (after starring at Methacton High and Oklahoma State University). But that day, the day he was born—that was an unforgettable day. My son was born, we beat the Giants, and I had three hits.

WRAPPING IT UP

It may seem dramatic or contrived (in reality, it's simply serendipitous), but the Phils picked up the pace right around that Friday the 13th. For whatever reason, they suddenly jelled and won two of the next three games and eight of the next nine en route to an 81–80 campaign.

As for the Wine's baby boy, Robby went on to a nice career on the diamond. After he played at Oklahoma State, he had a short stint ('86 and '87) with the Houston Astros. Today Robby Wine is the manager of the Penn State nine.

CHAPTER 2

GARY MATTHEWS

"I played in a number of memorable games for a few different teams," says Gary Matthews. "I remember I had a big two-home run game against Phil Niekro one time, but sure, the game I remember most is the last game of the 1983 NLCS against the Dodgers. I knocked in the game-winning runs with a homer."

MEET GARY MATTHEWS

Gary Nathaniel Matthews was drafted directly out of San Fernando High School in June 1968 by the San Francisco Giants. He made his first big-league appearance for the Giants on September 6, 1972. The next year, he won a starting job, giving the Giants a formidable outfield trio of Bobby Bonds, Garry Maddox, and Gary Matthews. The 22-year-old Californian batted .300 as a rookie Giant (ninth best in the NL) with 12 homers, 74 runs scored, and 17 stolen bases. His accomplishments earned him Rookie-of-the-Year honors.

Matthews attained the .300 plateau twice more in his career—once as a Brave in 1979 and once as a Phillie in 1981. He finished his career with a .282 average, 234 home runs, and 978 RBIs. On three different occasions, Matthews (aka 'the Sarge') finished in the top 25 in the MVP voting. He came closest to copping the prize in 1984 when, as a Cub, he finished fifth. Three of the top five '84 finishers were Cubs: Ryne Sandberg, Rick Sutcliffe (the winner and a former Phillie), and Matthews.

Gary played a few years in San Francisco. He was granted free agency after the '76 season and was signed by the Atlanta Braves. He enjoyed perhaps his finest years in Atlanta. The zenith of his career came in 1979, when he slammed a career-best 27 homers (his second-highest seasonal total was 21), batted a career-high .304, and drove in a career-high 90 runs. That year, he exceeded the .500 slugging percentage mark for a full season for the first and only time in his career.

In March 1981, the Braves dealt him to the Phillies for Bob Walk.

"That's where I got the name 'Sarge,'" Matthews reveals. "Pete Rose gave it to me. He said, 'You know, I think I should call you Sarge.' I thought about it for a minute and said, 'I like that name. Yeah, I'm the Sarge.' That was it. From then on, that's what I was—the Sarge."

In '81 as a Phillie, 'the Sarge' accounted for one-third of another productive outfield triumvirate as he teamed with Garry Maddox and Bake McBride. The Phils were going great guns until the baseball strike deflated their balloon. The Phillies played Montreal in the Divisional Series at the end of a checkered season. They buried themselves in a deep hole right off the bat, dropping the first two at Le Stade Olympique in Montreal in a best-of-five series. Philadelphia came back and won two at the Vet but in the rubber game, the Expos' Steve Rogers outdueled Hall of Famer Steve Carlton 3–0. The Sarge was the star of the series for the losers. Safe for Keith Moreland who had seven fewer at-bats, Sarge's .400 batting average substantially eclipsed all other Phillies, including Mike Schmidt, who hit a meager .250.

In 1983, Matthew's regular-season production dipped. Compared to the previous year, his batting average plummeted from .281 to .250. His runs scored declined from 89 to 66, and his RBIs dropped from 83 to 50. He made up for his relative lack of production when the NLCS rolled around. Matthews slammed three homers in four games. His three dingers accounted for more than half the Phillies' home runs and surpassed the total for the entire Dodger squad. He batted a lusty .429, which was topped only by Mike Schmidt's .467, who led everyone in hits with seven.

Meanwhile, the Phillies pitching staff compiled a miserly 1.03 ERA. Steve Carlton's ERA was an otherworldly 0.66. Unfortunately, the NLCS was the Phillies' last hurrah. In the World Series, they were embar-

"The Sarge," as Pete Rose nicknamed Gary Matthews, was the MVP of the 1983 NLCS. *Focus on Sport/Getty Images*

rassed by the Baltimore Orioles four games to one. Their .195 batting average (Schmidt hit a paltry .050) was most responsible for their failure.

In 1984, Gary Matthews, the NLCS MVP hero for Philadelphia, was shipped to Chicago along with Porfi Altamirano and Bob Dernier. The Phillies got Bill Campbell and Mike Diaz in return. It was not a good deal for the Phillies. Matthews responded with a .291 season with 14 homers for the Cubs, who made it all the way to the NLCS. The following year, the 34-year-old veteran started to slow down. He managed 21 homers in only 370 at-bats in 1986. However, in the middle of the following season, he had to pack his bags for Seattle. After a lone partial season in Seattle, the club granted him free agency. The Sarge called it quits.

His playing career terminated, Matthews worked in private industry for a few years before the Cubs organization hired him as their minor-league hitting instructor. He worked that job from 1995 to 1997. He was a major-league coach for the next seven years, performing those services for the Blue Jays, the Brewers, and the Cubs respectively. In 2007, Gary chose a respite remote from the diamond and teamed with the Phils broadcasting team.

Matthews and wife, Sandra, have four children—the aforementioned Gary Jr., Delvon, Dustin, and Dannon.

SETTING THE STAGE

The Phillies had what could be called an unconvincing season in '83. The team, dubbed the "Wheeze Kids," mirrored the protagonist in the movie *The Shootist*. The Phillies corralled a bunch of aging, end-of-the-road diamond legends onto one roster. The old guys mustered all their collective savvy and experience to win a division title and a National League Championship Series.

The '83 roster read like a who's who of the baseball stars of the seventies. The Phillies constellation of dimming stars could best be termed Red Giants or more accurately, former Red Giants. In 1983 for the Phillies, former Cincinnati Red, 42-year-old Pete Rose batted .245; 39-year-old Joe Morgan, .230; and 41-year-old Tony Perez, .241. Philly fans never really embraced the latter two, perhaps because they had been hated enemies for so long.

In 1983, the Phillies drew their lowest attendance since 1975, excluding the strike year of 1981, and attendance that year would have surpassed the '83 figure if 1981 had been a full season.

Moreover, Philly fans had grown used to their home-grown team of the seventies. Most of the Phillies stars of the seventies had come up through the Phillie system and enjoyed long, fruitful tenures in the Quaker City. They had woven themselves into the fabric of Quaker City life and lore. While fans envied Cincinnati talents like Morgan and Perez, when they were dominating baseball as the 'Big Red Machine,' these guys felt somewhat like hired guns to the average fan. Worse, these imports were hired guns at the end of their string, akin to the aging gunslinger John Wayne portrayed in *The Shootist*.

Even Matthews, who by '83 was a mainstay of the club, was a relative newcomer compared with recently departed stars like Luzinski, Boone, and Bowa. That trio gave its best years to the Phillies. In their stead, the fans watched outfielder Von Hayes (with un-Luzinski-esque stats: .265, six home runs), catcher Bo Diaz (.234 batting average) and Ivan DeJesus (.254) holding starting positions that had until recently been Philly institutions. The team had a scent of the unfamiliar which failed to dissipate.

The Phillies started the '83 season with their de rigeur opening-day loss as the Mets' Doug Sisk bested Steve Carlton 2–0 at Shea Stadium. On April 22, the Phillies climbed into first place for the first time. In a hotly contested race, they held on to the top spot off and on for a month. On May 23, Fernando Valenzuela shut them out 2–0 and the Phillies tumbled to third, where they mostly remained until John Denny pitched them back into first place on July 12. A week later, they were in third again.

It was a yo-yo season. No one team burst out of the pack. The three contenders—the Phillies, the Expos, and the Pirates all hovered slightly over the .500 mark. Then unexpectedly and suddenly in mid-September, the Phillies caught fire. Starting with a 13-inning, 3–2 victory over St. Louis, they reeled off 11 straight victories. Their timely skein nestled them comfortably in first place with a 4 1/2-game lead on September 26 and only five games left to play. The Phillies continued their winning ways after a lone setback by the Cubs that day. They ended up winning the division by six games.

The Phillies were headed to the NLCS once again. Like a bad dream, they had to face the hated Dodgers once again—the guys who, in the late seventies, had twice slammed the door to October glory in their faces.

The NLCS was a best-of-five affair in '83. The Dodgers were heavy favorites. Los Angeles had finished the regular season with only one more win than the Phillies. But in head-to-head competition, the

Phillies found themselves on the wrong side of a 1–11 log. On paper the NLCS looked like a horrendous mismatch.

The Dodger domination had run its course by that October. In game one at Dodger Stadium, Steve Carlton and Al Holland blanked their confident opponent. Mike Schmidt's first-inning homer (only the 16th *run* the Phillies tallied all season against Dodger hurlers in 13 games) was the game's sole score. In game two, Matthews got a home run in the second inning (for the 17th run scored against the Dodgers all season). His blast accounted for the Phillies' lone run as the Dodgers rolled to a 4–1 win and evened the series.

Now the scene shifted to Philadelphia's Veterans Stadium. In game three, Charles Hudson pitched a four-hitter. Matthews tagged two singles, hit another home run, and stole a base as the Phillies prevailed 7–2 to surge ahead 2–1 in the series. The Phillies needed one more win to earn their second trip to the World Series in three years.

THE GAME OF MY LIFE
OCTOBER 8, 1983
BY GARY MATTHEWS

I took great pleasure in beating the Dodgers. I'm an L.A. guy myself. I grew up out there, although I think my favorite city is San Francisco. I had another thing that motivated me. I knew the Dodgers had denied my teammates a couple of trips to the World Series, so beating them meant a lot to my teammates and Philly fans.

I felt good that series. I was seeing the ball and swinging well. We wanted to win that fourth game and not extend the series to five games. We had things going our way. Carlton was on the mound and we were playing at the Vet. This was the game to take care of business. The Dodgers were throwing Jerry Reuss at us, who was a tough left-hander, a big guy with good stuff.

The Dodgers started off with a single (Steve Sax) but Carlton picked him off. Dusty Baker, who was a really tough hitter, doubled, but Lefty pitched his way out of the inning without allowing a run. In our half, we got on the board right away. We did it with two outs too (Morgan opened the inning with a groundout, and Rose followed with a fly out to right). Then Schmidty singled and Sixto Lezcano singled. I stepped up to the plate and caught one good. I hit it out for a homer. We were out 3–0 in the first and the Vet was screaming.

Dusty Baker, who always managed to hurt us, homered in the Dodger fourth. That closed the gap to 3–1. We got a couple more in the fifth. I remember Schmidt doubled and I was intentionally walked—by the end of the inning we were up 5–1. Then in the sixth, we put the game out of reach, at least it was out of reach the way our pitchers were handling the Dodgers. Lezcano hit a two-run homer and we went up 7–1 with only three innings left. I think the Dodgers picked up another run in the seventh or eighth (the Dodgers scored one run in the eighth) but Al Holland (aka 'Mr. T') shut the door and we were on our way to the World Series.

WRAPPING IT UP

In the '83 World Series, the Phillies mimicked their NLCS start. They did not replicate the finish. They scored their only two runs on solo homers by Maddox and Morgan. Phillies' rival, the Baltimore Orioles, tallied a single run on a solo homer. The Phillies won 2–1 to jump out 1–0 in the Series.

Then their bats went silent—dead silent. Philadelphia dropped the next four straight. The Series ended ignominiously for Philadelphia when Scott MacGregor blanked them 5–0 in game five. The Phillies plated only nine runs in five games.

The following season brought a 50-percent change in the starting lineup (first base, Len Matuszek for Pete Rose; second base, Juan Samuel for Joe Morgan; Catcher, Ozzie Virgil for Bo Diaz; out-fielder Glenn Wilson for Gary Matthews). The Phillies tumbled down to fourth place. Attendance dropped as well, if only slightly (2,128,339 to 2,062,696). Attendance managed to creep over the two-million mark only twice in the ensuing decade, until the Beards, Bellies, and Biceps crew drew 3,137,674 raucous fans to south Philly to smash every Philly record for attendance.

CHAPTER 3

TERRY HARMON

Two games come to mind," says Terry Harmon, when asked for the game of his life. "The first was my major-league debut. I was down in Florida and got the call to report to the big club. Naturally, I was thrilled and a bit nervous. I flew up to Chicago to join the club and landed at about one in the morning. I was still groggy. I sat on the bench that game, trying to soak in the fact that I was in the Big Leagues. About the sixth or seventh inning, I got the call. I wasn't expecting it, but it came. They told me to grab a bat and pinch hit—I did. I went up against Ferguson Jenkins and singled. The rest of my career wasn't quite that successful.

"But as great a thrill as that first at-bat and first hit was, I'll pick another game as the game of my life. This one was in Chicago too. Jim Bunning was pitching for us. I guess my big games always managed to have some tie-in with a Hall of Fame pitcher. Anyway, this game means more and more to me as time goes by. I set a record for handling the most fielding chances in a single game for a second baseman. As time goes on, I realize, 'Hey, to have my name in the record book with all those great players—that's a pretty nice thing.'

MEET TERRY HARMON

Terry Walter Harmon was born in Toledo, Ohio.

"I like to say I made it to the bottom of the top," Terry chuckles. "I played for ten years—the entire time as a utility player. That's a long time to last up here for anyone. It's a *really* long time for a guy who never cracked a starting lineup."

Terry went to Ohio University—same as Mike Schmidt.

"I guess the similarity ends there," Harmon jokes.

He played in the minors for a few years before being called up to the Phillies for a cup of coffee in July 1967. He made his first appearance in the majors as a pinch runner but he was only in a couple of games before being sent down again. Terry returned to the Phillies for good in 1969. Terry never managed more than 221 at-bats in a single season. He did that in 1971 when he fashioned a respectable .284 average. He topped the .284 figure one time with a .295 mark in 1976, the year before his retirement. Terry finished his career with a modest .233 lifetime average.

Harmon did have some big days, particularly in his final season. On July 26 that year he spelled regular shortstop Larry Bowa in a doubleheader against the Dodgers. The game pitted the first-place Dodgers against the second-place Phillies in front of 47,966 people in Dodger Stadium. In game one, Steve Carlton was outdueled 5–1 by Rick Rhoden. The Phillies managed only six hits. Harmon had one of them. In game two, he had one of the finest days of his career at the plate as the Phillies turned the tables on L.A. behind Jim Lonborg and won 5–1. Terry went three for three with a walk, two runs scored, and two RBIs. He scored the go-ahead run to break a 1–1 deadlock and later iced the game with a two-run round-tripper.

Harmon's career spanned a period that began with a 1969 team that posted a 63–99 (.389) record and ended with a powerhouse 1977 squad that hammered out a 101–61 (.623) record.

As his longtime manager Danny Ozark observed long ago, "Terry is an important part of this team. Besides giving us solid defense and good base-running, Terry's a guy that any manager would like in his club-house. He's not out there doing something on the field every day but he's always contributing, always doing something for the good of the team."

SETTING THE STAGE

The shockwaves of the Gene Mauch era had still not stopped quaking in 1971.

Terry Harmon says, "I got to the bottom of the top," because he spent his 10-year career entirely as a utility player. *Photo by Brace Photography*

After a skein of six straight winning seasons under Mauch in the sixties, the Phillies hit the skids. Mauch left a 27–27 team in 1968. The Phillies ended the season at 76–86 under the successive regimes of George Myatt and Bob Skinner. The rapidity of regime changes put the squad in disarray. In '69, the Myatt-Skinner succession was reversed. Skinner started the season as the Phillies' skipper and Myatt finished it. The Phillies slumped to an abysmal 63–99 (.389) record. Frank Lucchesi was named manager in 1970. He held the post for three years. Lucchesi added stability but little else, and the team's performance failed to improve.

The '70 Phillies finished fifth. By 1971, the stalwarts of the '64 Phillies—Johnny Callison, Tony Gonzalez, Wes Covington, Cookie Rojas—were all gone. The 1964 pitching duo of Chris Short and Jim Bunning was reunited. Bunning had spent the previous two campaigns in Pittsburgh and LA. However, the once-feared duo was now a mere shadow of what it once was. The new staff ace was Rick Wise who went on to a 17–14 season in '71. Wise and Woody Fryman were the only Phillies pitchers with at least two decisions who managed winning records.

On April 11, 1971, the Phillies' two-game winning streak, which came on the heels of a two-game losing streak to start the campaign, afforded them one of their final opportunities of the season for .500-or-better team status. As of April 16, they never had another chance to win a game. Their season was, as they say, all downhill from there. One of the lasting beauties of the national pastime, however, is that a few bright spots always manage to penetrate the gatherings of dark clouds. For the '71 Phillies, one of those bright spots occurred quietly on June 12.

By the time June 12 rolled around, as noted, the Phillies were not enjoying their finest days—ditto for their game-day opponents, the San Diego Padres. June 12 was one of those rare days in June, warm and comfortable. However, only 17,039 showed up at the ballpark. The hometown ennui owed to the Phillies poor showing. Already, the Phillies were 12 ½ games behind first-place Pittsburgh. Philadelphia was buried deep in the basement, three games behind the fifth-place Expos in the six-team NL East. In the West, the Padres' were even deeper in the cellar, 19 ½ games behind the pace-setting Giants. Even in games that are meaningless in terms of the pennant race, records can be set—Terry Harmon set one that day.

THE GAME OF MY LIFE

JUNE 12, 1971

BY TERRY HARMON

I'll bet you haven't had many guys in this book pick a game where they went hitless as the game of their life. I went hitless in this game. Actually, the real hero of the game was Jim Bunning. Everyone knew Bunning was a great pitcher. He was 39 years old at the time, but the guy could still be tough with his slider as long as he had location. Well, Bunning was on that day. It was a night game. Saturday games weren't all automatically night games in those days. I remember it was a quick game (completed in 2:05 hours) and Jim was so sharp, he didn't give anybody anything to hit. That's why he threw so many ground balls. For some reason, most of them came my way.

I didn't touch the ball in the first inning although I think there was a ground-out. Bunning fielded one that came back to the mound and tossed it to first for the game's first assist. In the second inning, I got my first assist. I had a few good stops that night, but nothing that stands out in my mind as spectacular. One thing I remember—usually when I started, I hit way down in the lineup at the number-eight slot. That night I led off. I went hitless (0–4), but it was gratifying to be at a key slot in the batting order. You wouldn't know from our won-lost record, but we did have some good ballplayers like Tim McCarver, Willie Montanez, Deron Johnson, and of course, a young Larry Bowa.

We scored early. I struck out in our half of the first, but the ball got by the catcher, Bob Barton. Then their outfielder (left fielder Bobby Pfeil) muffed a fly ball—the Padres were having their problems. We ended up bunching a few hits and scoring a few runs. The Phillies tallied all three of the game's runs in the first inning. After that, it settled down into an old-fashioned pitching duel and Bunning came out on top.

From the second inning on it seemed like I was involved in something every time we took the field. I was focused on the game and wasn't aware of the record at all. I think the announcers were. In the last inning, I handled three straight grounders, one-two-three and the game was over. It's funny, my teammates seemed to know about the record but I didn't. Bunning had such a great game. He didn't strike many out (he fanned three and reliever Bucky Brandon fanned two), but that's why I got so many chances. Bunning kept the Padres from getting any wood on the ball.

WRAPPING IT UP

The Phillies wobbled through the rest of the season and finished at 67–95—good for a sixth-place finish in the NL East. Jim Bunning finished the campaign at 5–12, with a 5.48 ERA. He called it quits after that season. However, Larry Bowa staked a permanent place on the squad. Meanwhile, the Phillies brought a chunky kid named Luzinski up for a late-season look. Rick Wise went on to pitch a no-hitter later that season (and slam two homers in the same game to boot). Those kinds of Wise performances enticed St. Louis to fork up a hurler named Steve Carlton for Wise in the off-season. By the end of '71, the foundation of the Phillies' seventies juggernaut had started to take shape.

Harmon looks back with pleasure on his major league career.

"I was fortunate," he notes. "I had a long career in major league baseball, which is a terrific 'job' to have. Since my playing days, I've been working in the cable-television industry. In 1977, I hooked up with Prism and worked with them for four or five years. Then I worked with QVC for 15 years. I retired from QVC in 2000 and started working for Jewelry TV—yeah, 24 hours of on-air jewelry sales. Last year, we did about $500 million in sales. I'm the guy who knocks on the doors of cable operators and tries to get our channel in their distribution. All in all, I've had a fortunate life, and my years with the Phillies were the greatest."

CHAPTER 4

TOMMY GREENE

"When you asked me to think about the game of my life," says Tommy Greene. "I figured all the fans would figure I'd pick one of two games. I'd pick either my no-hitter or one of the many important games I pitched in 'The Phillies Year' of 1993. I'll admit, the pennant-clinching game was one game I considered. When we beat the Braves and Mitch came in and put them down one-two-three in the ninth, you know *that* had to be special. The games that year were special because we had such a great group of guys on that team.

"But the game I think was the game of my life came the game *after* my no-hitter. I threw the no-hitter against the Expos in Montreal. The next time I pitched was in Philly against the Expos again. It was sort of a validation game. It sort of put the stamp on the no-hitter as being for real. I think that was the game of my life, strange as it might seem. I gained respect as a professional, and that's something everyone who comes up here (to the majors) is fighting for."

MEET TOMMY GREENE

Ira Thomas Greene was born in Lumberton, North Carolina. Early on, he showed promise as a pitcher, which turned out to be a mixed blessing.

"I had a tremendous growth spurt when I was young," Tommy reflects. "I shot up from 5-foot-7 to 6-foot-2 from June to February of my sophomore year in high school. That was the cause of all my problems, but I found that out too late. I shouldn't have pitched my sophomore year but I did. My arm was so bad that my dad had to drive me up to Richmond to see a sports medicine specialist. The doctor, a guy named Packer—this guy was about 6-foot-10—X-rayed my shoulder. He didn't like what he saw. The condition was something he usually found in hips, not in shoulders. That's because the hip is weight-bearing. The shoulder is not. The way Dr. Packer explained it, I was basically trying to throw with a broken arm. He said I would have to choose one of two options to try to heal it. One, he could put a pin through it and try to get everything lined up properly. If he did that, I wouldn't be able to pitch again. Or I could do nothing. But I had to avoid using the arm for a long while. As he explained it, even if I fell face down, I wasn't supposed to break my fall with my right arm!

"I did pitch every year in high school. I was totally a fastball pitcher. My high school coach called all the pitches my freshman and sophomore year. He was a good coach. He didn't overpitch me and hurt me. My problems, like I said, were basically from repetitive use, not overuse, if you know what I mean. The physical condition I had due to growth set me up for the future problems.

"I didn't throw a breaking ball in high school. As a pitcher, I was all about placement of the fastball—even after I learned how to throw a breaking ball. Everything stems from the fast ball. Leo Mazzone is the one who showed me how to throw the breaking ball when I came up in the Braves organization. No one ever showed me a changeup. When the hitters got on my fast ball, I'd spin one into them. Otherwise, I was always trying to put that fastball in the right place."

The Braves, flashing their ever-vigilant eye for pitching talent, drafted Greene on the first round, 14th pick overall, of the 1985 draft. The young pitcher was brought up to the parent club in 1989. He started four games and ended with a 1–2 record. The following year he was 1–0 (though with a very un-Atlanta-ish 8.03 ERA) when he was dealt to the Phillies on August 9. Tommy was the "player to be named later" when Dale Murphy was dealt to Philadelphia for Jeff Parrett. For the '90 Phillies, Greene started seven games and posted a 2–3 record with a 4.15 ERA.

Tommy Greene was a vital cog on the pitching staff for the pennant-winning 1993 Phillies. *MLB Photos via Getty Images*

"Every player is different," Tommy explains. "When I was coming up through the Braves' system, I was a passive, easygoing, kind of gullible guy. I had to learn to light that proverbial 'fire in the belly' and I did. Coming up in the Braves system and working with Leo Mazzone, I learned how to establish the plate as mine—not the batter's."

When Greene was a young Braves pitcher, David Justice set him up with his future wife (i.e., *Greene's* future wife, not David Justice's future wife, who happened to be Halle Berry. They were married from 1992 to 1996).

"David told me I've got the perfect woman for you," Greene proudly says. "He was right. From the moment I met Lorie, that was it. We eventually got married and we've been happy ever since. She was my rock during all my rehabilitation for my shoulder."

Early in 1991, shortly after he turned 24 years of age, Greene left his mark in baseball history. He accomplished what a trio of Phillie Hall of Famers, which was what Grover Cleveland Alexander, Robin Roberts, and Steve Carlton had all failed to do. Greene became only the eighth Phillies hurler to toss a no-hitter, and only the fourth in the modern, post-1920 era. He finished the season with a 13–7 record and a 3.38 ERA. Greene appeared destined for stardom. However, arm problems plagued him in 1992 and cut his production down to 64 ⅓ innings, a drastic dip from the 207 ⅔ innings he toiled the season before.

Then came 1993. "That was the 'Phillie season' as I call it," he says smiling. "That year was all about consistency. The hitters picked up the pitchers when we sagged and vice versa. That was my best year ever for baseball. I had the most fun. It was a special time for every player on that squad. Philly fans respected the way we played. They related to our style of play and hustle. Mitch called us a band of 'gypsies, tramps, and thieves.' We were in our own world, like one big family."

After 1993, Greene would only pitch 78 ⅓ more major league innings.

"In the early eighties with my growth plates slipping, I didn't have the flexibility to endure," he recounts with pain. "From age 15 to 30, it was like putting a clicker on me. I only had so many pitches in me because of those physical problems. All those problems caught up to me after '93."

Tommy struggled through pain in 1995 in a dismal 0–5, 8.29 season. Injuries forced him to sit out the entire '96 campaign.

Following that season, the Phillies granted him free agency. The Astros took a chance on Greene and signed him in February '97. He worked only nine innings that season. It was his final. The Braves picked him up, but Tommy never made another major-league appearance. Injuries had terminated his baseball career at age 30.

"In '98, I wound up getting surgery on my shoulder," Tommy explains. "That was kind of the last leg of a long journey. At that point, I had gotten so bad that I couldn't even play catch with my son in the backyard. I couldn't push open a door. I had two previous surgeries on my shoulder but those procedures were really fixing the wrong thing. They were rotator-cuff operations that corrected tears and inflammation. They weren't fixing the real cause, which went back to those ninth-grade problems. At the end, I was pitching in pain all the time. You expect to pitch in pain at times, but you can't pitch in pain all the time—that's where I was though. The doctor I went to at Duke confirmed that my problems stemmed from those injuries as a kid—a slipped epithesis as they call it. When I threw, I lost internal rotation. My shoulder wouldn't roll through the motion. It would basically stop and slide.

"I actually learned to pitch smarter when I was hurt," he explains. "I had fewer punch-outs and fewer walks but my arm was killing me all the time. I couldn't even pick up a ball in between starts.

"I went through a long rehab. I gave it everything I had. I wanted to stay in the game so bad. The whole thing taught me a lot. I never realized how much I learned all those years in baseball. That's why I try to help young kids now. I love to share my experience with young guys who are chasing the same dream I did about playing big-league ball.

"Looking back, the only thing I would like to change is how I handled my shoulder problems when I was young. I wish I hadn't pitched American-Legion ball when I was a 15-year-old high school freshman. I'd like to see how my career would have turned out if I hadn't. I have no regrets about my career itself. I did all I could to stay in the game. I worked hard in the off-season to stay in shape. It just wasn't meant to be.

"My son Seth, our only child, is pitching and playing first base now. He's a young sophomore. He'll graduate at 17 and physically he's still growing. He's about 6-foot-1, 175 pounds, which is smaller than I was in high school. I graduated at 6-foot-5 and about 230 pounds. At this point as a pitcher, all Seth cares about is velocity. I tell him, 'Watch Curt Schilling pitch. Watch how he doesn't throw his hardest every pitch. Good pitchers throw most of their pitches with about 90 percent effort. Then at a crucial point in the game when they really need it, they reach back for something extra. That's what Schilling does. He throws about 91 mph until he needs something extra. Then he humps up and brings it at about 96 mph. That's what you should try to imitate—that's pitching."

SETTING THE STAGE

"Every time a guy throws a no-hitter, the media starts buzzing about Johnny Vander Meer," Greene philosophizes. "Vander Meer threw two consecutive no-hitters in the thirties or forties. He's the only guy who ever managed two no-hitters in a row. I had no-hit the Expos late in May (the 23rd). They had some guys who could really swing a bat like Andres Galarraga, Larry Walker, Tim Wallach, Marquis Grissom, and Delino DeShields. I walked seven guys in that no-hitter. I also struck out ten. After the game, because of those seven walks, some of the Expos said I wasn't 'pitching to them.' That wasn't true. I *was* pitching. I just wasn't giving into them. That's what pitching is. Even when I had three balls on them, I wouldn't come in with anything good to hit.

"I didn't read the sport pages too much in my playing days. The reporters in Philly are the ones who told me what the Expos were saying. That gave me a lot of incentive. I wanted another shot to kind of validate my no-hitter. The opportunity came fast—on my next start.

"As for the sportswriters, I had a good relationship with Paul Hagen. Paul was always a straight shooter with me. When I asked that something be kept off the record, he kept it that way. I never liked to express anything unprofessional to the reporters and Paul respected that.

"It's funny. After the no-hitter, I don't think I fully gained confidence right away. That's why the next game was so important. Terry Mulholland helped my confidence. He threw the last Phillie no-hitter before mine (on August 15, 1990 against the Giants). Terry advised me, 'Throwing a no-hitter is a big steppingstone toward believing in yourself. Now, you've got to let yourself take that step!' But I worried. I was a young guy at that point. I wanted consistency. I didn't want my no-hitter to be a flash in the pan. After the high of one ballgame like that, it's natural for a young pitcher to start wondering how well he'll do the next time he takes the mound. The way things turned out was great. I had the ultimate test. I was going up against the same team. They had a lot to prove and so did I."

THE GAME OF MY LIFE
OCTOBER 1, 1976
BY TOMMY GREENE

I matched up against 'Oil Can' Boyd. He had his best years with Boston (1976 was Oil Can's final year in the majors), but he could still bring it. As for me, I shortstopped any comparisons to Johnny Vander Meer real quick. The leadoff man, Delino DeShields lined a single to center. He tried to steal and Darrin Fletcher, who was catching for us that night, gunned him down. Then Grissom doubled and stole third. I punched the next guy out (Ivan Calderon). Ron Hassey grounded out and I was out of the inning. The Expos didn't put another guy on base until the sixth inning.

We went down in the first. I think Krukker worked a walk. That guy was amazing—the way he could work a pitcher. In the second, Rickie Jordan hit a solo homer. That was all I needed but we ended up getting a lot more.

Dave Martinez singled in the fifth with two out. But I got the next guy to ground out and I was out of the inning. We came back with a big inning and jumped out 6–0. I think we had a big homer (Fletcher hit a three-run blast) in the middle innings and, at that point, I was completely comfortable. The fans were totally into the game. It seems like we had a lot of fans there, compared to the number at the Montreal game (there were nearly twice as many at the Vet that night, 16,850—there were 8,833 in Montreal's Stade Olympique). Fletcher drove in a few more runs a couple of innings later. Then, in the bottom of the eighth, we got a couple more and blew them out. I put them down one-two-three in each of the final three innings.

The big thing this time around was that I didn't walk anyone. I had nine punch-outs and I felt in control the whole game long. The big thing I learned from this game was to throw strikes early in the game. If I did that, I didn't have to throw strikes later in the game. The batters start chasing anything close to the plate and the umpires start calling all the borderline pitches strikes.

When a pitcher gets control of the game and the strike zone, he can use the whole strike zone. I started games off by pitching down—

down and away. When I was in control of the game, once I established that I could pitch down, it enabled me to start pitching up. Really, the key thing about pitching is to change the batter's eye level. I'd start out throwing a few low pitches and getting the hitter to lean out over the plate chasing the ball. Then I'd come in chest high. The ball looks good to a hitter but he can't adjust. He can't catch up to it. That's the way I was pitching that night against Montreal. I learned a lot that night. I also gained a lot of confidence—two straight shutouts against a good hitting team. It doesn't get better for a pitcher.

WRAPPING IT UP

"I had two goals when I was coming up in the minors," continues Greene. "One was to make it into major-league baseball. The other goal was to get ten years under my belt once I did make it to the big leagues. I wanted to get fully vested as a major leaguer. I came close on that second goal but I didn't quite make it. I played eight years. I'm two years shy of being vested. I hope to get back to MLB in some capacity and stay for a couple more years—well, at least for a couple more years. I purposely chose to get away from baseball when I retired. I wanted to spend time with my family. It seemed like I was always away from the family during my playing days. That's the life of a baseball player. Getting out of the game at a young age gave me an opportunity to be with my family. I've really enjoyed it. But in a few years, I'd like to get back and coach. And yes, I'd love to come back to Philadelphia."

CHAPTER 5

DAVE HOLLINS

"Certainly the biggest game I played in was the sixth game of the NLCS against the Braves in 1993," says Dave Hollins. "But you're asking me to pick the game of my life, the game I remember most. Well, that game against the Braves—that's the game. I hit the homer off Maddox that night. In terms of satisfaction and excitement, I guess it doesn't get much better than that."

MEET DAVE HOLLINS

David Michael Hollins grew up in Buffalo, New York—a town noted for its harsh, relentless winters. That's kind of how Hollins played the game of baseball—with a harsh and uncompromising coldness. "David was like a linebacker wearing a baseball glove," says Jim Fregosi. "He ran the bases like a linebacker. Nothing was going to stop him from being safe at any base he was headed for. In fact, David might have been the finest baserunner I've ever seen going from first to third on a single."

Hollins starred in baseball and football at Orchard Park High School in Buffalo. After his graduation in '84, he played at the University of South Carolina. The San Diego Padres selected Hollins in the sixth round of the 1987 amateur draft. The Phillies alertly nabbed him in the 1989 Rule 5 draft. Hollins quickly became noted for his intensity.

"I remember Dave so well when he first came up," says Don Carman. "He would pace. He wasn't playing much and he couldn't stand sitting on the bench. I kept telling him his time would come. Well his time did come and he made the most of it when the opportunity came along."

John Kruk probably captured more media attention than any of his '93 Phillies mates—a crew that became national darlings with their eccentric, free-spirited approach to the Grand Old Game. However, when you talk with the warriors themselves—the guys on the field that year—it's quite possible Dave Hollins inspires more tales and stories than anyone.

"You couldn't get within ten feet of Head's (Hollins') locker before a game," recalls Pete Incaviglia. He just sat there staring at it, kind of mumbling to himself. After the game, he did the same thing. If he had a bad game, nobody got near him. I'll never forget this one day when Dave had played a horrible game. I think he made an error and also made the final out of the game. Whatever he did, he did not play a good game. He came into the clubhouse and tore the place apart. Then he just sat in front of his locker. Nobody in the whole clubhouse would say a word. Finally Kruk broke the silence. He walked over to Dave's locker and said for all to hear, 'Man, you really suck!' We all broke up. Hollins broke up. The clubhouse was our refuge that year, and Dave played a unique role."

Hollins was willing to endure any pain and take whatever measures were necessary to benefit his team. That's why he led the league and set a Phillies franchise record in the process, by getting hit by pitched balls 19 times in '92.

"David had this habit of leaning out over the plate," Fregosi explains. "He wouldn't back off and concede an inch to a pitcher. And he would never give any pitcher the pleasure of acknowledging pain. Dave never rubbed the area where he was plunked. He simply made his way stoically down to first and glowered at the pitcher all the way down."

The '93 Phillies remember him most for his intensity and concentration on his craft.

"Dave Hollins is the only guy I've ever seen that I think was actually capable of killing someone on the diamond," says Curt Schilling. He is quoted elsewhere as saying, "Dave Hollins is pretty intense even when he sleeps. He chews bricks."

1993 Phillies skipper Jim Fregosi calls "Headley," Dave Hollins, the most intense player he's ever seen. *Jonathan Daniel/Getty Images*

After his two terrific seasons in Philly, Hollins engaged a peripatetic path that led him to seven different clubs over the next seven seasons.

"I think Dave was never the same after that '93 season not only because of injuries, but because he had Phillie withdrawal syndrome," explains Pete Incaviglia, a '93 mate of Hollins. "I had it and so did a few others. Honest, baseball was never more fun than it was that year. We all felt that way. I was never in a clubhouse where the whole team was so intense and serious and dedicated to winning and yet had so much fun at the same time. I couldn't wait to get to the ball park every day. In fact, when I saw Joe Carter's home run going over the fence that night in Toronto—I wasn't mad at Mitch. Hell, Mitch left everything he had on the field every time he took the mound. No, I was sad because we wouldn't be coming to the ballpark the next day. I was sad because that season was ending. The intensity and joy that year—well, it was so great, I think the careers of Dave and me and others suffered. We were always looking to match that kind of atmosphere and we never again found it."

"I know there are lots of Dave Hollins stories out there," chuckles Hollins. "I was a young kid when I was in Philly. I reacted to the pressure the only way I knew by concentrating and playing tougher and trying harder. Sometimes my approach came across the wrong way. That's why I was happy to have the opportunity to come back to the Phillies in 2002 when Larry Bowa asked me. There were so many people I wanted to show a different side of me to. I wasn't the way people thought I was when they met me as a young guy. But all in all, my career was fulfilling. And now I'm scouting up here not far from my home in Buffalo so things are going well."

SETTING THE STAGE

Hollins started building up for the big game on October 13, 1993—a year before the game was actually played. That statement requires another "Dave Hollins story" told by John Kruk.

"This happened after the '92 season," remembers Kruk. "Dave and I were in Las Vegas. We ran into Greg Maddux and Steve Avery. "Head" saw Maddux across the room and walked over to him. Head said, 'Look, if you ever hit me or one of my teammates again, I'm going to kill you.' Then Dave walked away.

Maddux and I were in a cab the next day. Hollins was a new guy in the league at that point, not well established. Anyway, Maddux finally says to me, 'That guy Hollins—what was up with him? He wasn't serious, was he?' I said to Greg, 'Oh yeah, he's serious all right—about as serious as a heart attack.' Maddux never hit Hollins again. I don't blame Greg. I'd rather fight Mike Tyson without his medication than fight Dave Hollins."

Hollins chuckles at the story.

"Yeah, I was a little aggressive in those days," he adds. "But I think I set the record for getting hit in '92 and I wanted to serve notice to pitchers around the league. I never liked the Braves either when I played. I always felt like they acted like they were better than anyone—like we didn't belong on the same field with them. I used to purposely crowd the plate to show them I wasn't going to give in to them."

The Phillies started off the NLCS in '93 with a win behind Curt Schilling. They dropped the next two contests, only to come back with a 2–1 victory behind Danny Jackson, who pitched the game of his life. Tied at two games apiece, Schilling and Avery, the first-game starters hooked up again. Lenny Dykstra stroked a tenth-inning homer to break a 3–3 deadlock, while Larry Andersen came in for his first and only save of the season as the Phillies took the series lead three games to two.

In game number six, played at the Vet, the Braves' ace Greg Maddux was going up against Tommy Greene. All of Philadelphia was waiting for their Phillies to take them to the World Series for the first time since 1980.

THE GAME OF MY LIFE
OCTOBER 13, 1993
BY DAVE HOLLINS

I think I had a lifetime batting average of under .200 at that point against Maddox. I managed to hit Tom Glavine a little, but I wasn't as strong from the left side of the plate as I was from the right side. I think that's the main reason I had more success against Glavine than Maddux. Both those guys were tough.

The crowd pumped me up that night. The fans were screaming. They smelled blood. We needed one more win to take the NLCS and this was going to be the night. They were really into the game (there were 62,502 at the Vet that night and they watched the 1983 NLCS MVP Gary Matthews throw out the first ball).

The game got off great for us. Mickey Morandini, batting second, rocketed one off Maddox' leg. Maddox wasn't Maddox that night and I think it was because Mickey's shot altered his motion.

John Kruk adds, "Leo Mazzone, the Braves' pitching coach told me later that Mickey's ball hit Greg solid in the right calf and Maddux had a tough time pushing off on that leg the rest of the night. Something was wrong. You don't score six runs of Maddux on a normal night."

We didn't score in the first couple of innings but we were working Maddux—making him pitch. That '93 team did that better than any team I've ever seen. We'd take pitches, work walks and get the starters out early, then feast on the middle relief. In the third, we bunched walks and hits, moved some runners and then Dutch Daulton got the first big hit of the night. The bases were loaded and he unloaded with a double. Then in the home half of the fifth, Mickey got on base on an error and I put one out—a monster 422-foot blast.

That was probably my biggest hit ever. Maddux has that tough change-up and he never got it working all night. It normally ran in on left-handers. But the one he threw me was flat. He left it up and over the plate and it just kind of stopped. I saw it all the way and got good wood on it.

The next inning, Mickey got another big hit (a two-run triple) that put us on top 6–1. We knew we had them at that point. We were doing so good that night that Mitch came in and put them down in order in the ninth. It doesn't get better than that."

WRAPPING IT UP

One other name keeps popping up in that big October 13 game—Mickey Morandini. Interestingly, Mickey was a bit of a surprise starter that night. Fregosi gave the Mick the nod over Mariano Duncan who had platooned all year with Mickey at second base.

"I put Mickey in there because he had lots of success against Maddux," Fregosi explains. "Mariano struggled a little."

The stats bear out Fregosi's hunch. Morandini boasted a .359 lifetime average (14 for 39) against Maddux at that point as contrasted with Mariano's .172 average (5 for 29).

Fregosi's hunch panned out. Morandini's line drive off Maddux' calf was a key factor in the game—as was his two-run triple. He played one of the finest games ever played for someone who only went 1 for 5 at the plate.

As for Dave Hollins, 15 years after the '93 glory days, he says, "I've got a little medical situation with diabetes but it's under control. It's all about diet. If I eat properly, the diabetes is under control. I work out about three or four times a week lifting weights. I'm in good shape and I've added a lot of cardio exercises to my routine.

"I like working for the Orioles—I really do. This is only my second year out of uniform but it's a good transition for me. I'm home a lot more often. You don't get much time at home with the kids when you're playing ball or coaching. I've got five kids now—two boys and three girls. So I'm enjoying getting home with them and watching them grow."

Here's another tidbit about that big victory, and Dave Hollins' finest hour, that sent the Phillies to their fourth World Series. That win balanced the ledger a bit. On the same unlucky date (October 13) back in 1915, the Boston Red Sox on the power of Harry Hoover's two home runs, won the 1915 World Series four games to one over the Phillies in front of 20,306 disappointed Phillies fans.

CHAPTER 6

JACK BALDSCHUN

"I had both a save and a decision in a doubleheader," says Jack Baldschun, pondering his most momentous game in a Phillies uniform. "But one time I got a couple of wins in a doubleheader. It's tough to remember now how it all went. I know against Pittsburgh I pitched in both ends of a doubleheader. I believe I won the opener and saved the second game. But against St. Louis, I got both wins in the doubleheader. That's a pretty memorable accomplishment."

MEET JACK BALDSCHUN

Jack Edward Baldschun was born in Greenville, Ohio, on October 16, 1936. He played college ball one year (1955) for the University of Miami Hurricanes. In 1956, he left Miami after the Washington Senators signed him as a free agent. He came to the Phillies in the Rule 5 draft via the Minnesota Twins, who were known as the Washington Senators until 1960.

Baldschun arrived in Philly in 1961. He made an immediate impact. In his rookie year, he led all National League pitchers in games pitched with 65 and boasted a 5–3 won-lost record. His respectable ERA of 3.82 that season would be his highest as a Phillie. Twice, his ERA sank like his baffling screwball under 3.00.

Baldschun registered 12–7 and 11–7 records over the next two seasons. In each of those campaigns, he finished second in the senior circuit in games pitched. In Philly's ill-fated, 1964 meltdown season,

Jack ranked third in games pitched. The following year he placed fourth in the category.

"I lived on my screwball," explains Baldschun. "I came up with it when I was in Nashville in the minors. I kept experimenting. I was throwing to Dick Kennedy. I threw him a traditional screwball and then changed it a little and wound up with a pitch that either broke down and in like a screwball or down and out like a slider. It's tough to explain. Willie Mays once asked me if I ever gave anyone a pitch to hit. He told me he never got one from me. Willie said all my pitches start out over the plate and then dive into a zone where the batter never gets a good swing at them. 'The bottom drops out,' that's the way Willie put it. And Paul Waner, a Hall of Famer, once told me that the only other screwball he ever saw like mine was Carl Hubbell's. Waner added that Hubbell was the one guy he could never hit.

"When I started throwing that screwball in the minors, the other teams all accused me of throwing a spitter," Baldschun continues. "My screwball moved like a spitter. It's not that I didn't know how to throw a spitter too—I could. I just didn't throw it. I didn't have to. My screwball broke just as well. Sometimes in the minors, they threw wet towels out onto the field—you know, suggesting that I was wetting the ball up.

"I was a starter in the minors. I got to the big leagues and never started a game. In my entire big-league career, I never started at all. Gene Mauch was a friend of my minor-league coach. That's how Mauch got interested in me, and that's why he brought me over to Philadelphia in the first place.

"When I got to Philadelphia, Mauch called me into his office and said, 'I'm sure you could win me 15 games if you started. But you're too valuable to me coming out of the bullpen. Gene used me a lot— I liked that. I thrived on work. I think I might have the record for most games pitched in my first five years. Somebody told me that once. I pitched in 71 games in '64 and they asked me if I thought I could pitch more. I told them I could pitch in 100 games if I had to. I would like to have started every four days or so and then in between, pitch out of the bullpen. They wouldn't let me do that though.

"One time, I was working on some sort of a record for consecutive appearances. I think I had appeared in seven straight games and eight straight would have set a record. Chris Short was pitching

Jack Baldschun was one of the NL's most reliable workhorses in the Sixties.
Photo by Brace Photography

against the Dodgers and in the first three innings he got in trouble. I was warming up and set to go in for him, but Style (that's what Short's nickname was) pitched himself out of trouble every time. He got in trouble in the sixth too, and got out of it again. He ended up pitching a complete game, so I didn't get the record. Mauch knew about the record. He was set to put me in but Short didn't give him the opportunity. There's more to that story. Do you remember Chuck Connors in a TV show called 'The Rifleman?' Well, the Phillies were playing in California where they filmed the show and the people from the show invited me to the lot where they filmed it. They told me I would be on one of the episodes if I set that record. They asked me if I knew how to ride a horse. I told them I could learn. But as it turned out, I didn't get the record and didn't get on the show."

After the '65 season, the Phillies traded Baldschun to the Baltimore Orioles for Jackie Brandt and Darold Knowles. He never threw a pitch for the O's. They packaged Jack with Milt Pappas and Dick Simpson in a deal with the Cincinnati Reds that history chronicles as one of baseball's more one-sided deals. The Reds surrendered Frank Robinson who went on to MVP honors in Baltimore while Jack spent two disappointing seasons with the Reds.

Inked as a free agent by the newly franchised San Diego Padres, Jack went on to his finest won-lost record (7–2) in 1969 while appearing in 61 games. The following year, however, his appearances dropped off drastically to 12. Jack called it quits after the season.

Baldschun toyed with the idea of becoming a pitching coach. His wife did not second that emotion. Consequently Jack entered the working world. Imagine that—a big star needing to work and earn money to support himself after a baseball career. He became a salesman in the lumber industry for 25 years. Currently, the Baldschuns own a 15-acre farm near Green Bay (Sadly, he is a Packer fan).

SETTING THE STAGE

The 1963 season started off promising for the Philly nine. In the opener, skipper Gene Mauch handed the ball to Art Mahaffey, the staff ace at the time. Mahaffey was an NL All-Star for the Phillies in both 1961 and 1962. He squared off against Cincinnati's Joey Jay, who won 21 games in each of the previous two campaigns. Perhaps Jay's greatest claim to fame was becoming the first little league grad to play in the big leagues. While still an active pitcher, Jay wrote a magazine piece, "Don't Trap Your Son in Little League Madness"—where Joey blasted that Little League.

Mahaffey bested Jay 2–1. The following day, Ray Culp beat San Francisco 10–7. On Saturday, the Phillies dropped their first game of the season to the Cardinals and Curt Simmons, who shut out Mahaffey and the Phillies 7–0.

April 14 pitted the 2–1 Phillies against the 2–1 Cardinals in the season's first doubleheader.

THE GAME OF MY LIFE
APRIL 14, 1963
JACK BALDSCHUN

I guess this is more like the day of my life, not the game of my life, since I'm talking about two games.

I picked up an easy win in the first game. Chris Short was cruising along with a 3–0 lead going into the home half of the eighth. Then the Cards struck. They had a tough lineup: Curt Flood, Bill White, Stan Musial, Ken Boyer, and Dick Groat—not too many outs in that group. They hit a couple of triples and a single to come within one run of us (3–2) going into the ninth. In the ninth, Mauch let Short bat, something the current generation of young fans have never seen.

Chris struck out to lead off the inning. We followed with a couple of hits but didn't score, so all we had to do was keep them scoreless in the ninth and we won—That didn't happen. Chris James homered to lead off the inning and we were in a tie game, with prospects of losing. St. Louis put men on second and third with two out and Mauch called me in from the pen to face Curt Flood. I got him to hit the ball in the dirt to end the inning.

In the top of the tenth, Bobby Shantz came in for the Cards. We got a hit, a walk, and an intentional walk to load the bases. I was due up next. Earl Averill pinch hit for me and hit a sacrifice fly for the go-ahead run. That's the only run we got but it was all we needed.

In the bottom of the tenth, Jack Hamilton came in and set St. Louis down one-two-three. He got the save and I got the win—not bad for one-third of an inning's work.

Then came game two. Marcellino Lopez started for us. Lopez was a young kid—only 19 years old at the time. He started off wild, walking the first two batters before he got somebody out on a fly ball. But the cleanup batter, Ken Boyer doubled and Mauch had seen enough. He yanked Lopez and brought in Ray Culp, who was a real fireballer. Third baseman Don Hoak made an infield error by on the first play and St. Louis ended up scoring, so we were down 3–0 after the first inning.

It seemed like the Cards kept threatening the whole game and we kept inserting pitchers. After Culp, Jack Hamilton and Johnny Klippstein came on in relief, but the Cards didn't score. We held off each threat. Meanwhile, Ray Sadecki was mowing us down until the seventh inning. That inning, he got the first two guys out, but then he gave up a single before Tony Taylor hit a two-run homer that let us creep to within one run.

In the eighth, Don Demeter hit a big homer to tie the game. We kept going after that, stringing a bunch of singles together that put us ahead by a run. Mauch inserted me at that point with a one-run lead. I set the Cards down in order in the eighth. In the ninth, we added an insurance run. In the St. Louis half, I can't recall. They may have gotten a hit, but they didn't score. We came out on top 5–3 and I had my second win of the day and the season."

WRAPPING IT UP

Baldschun owned half of the first-place Phillies' wins at the close of business that first baseball Sunday of 1963. His ERA was a sterling 0.00. It was to be the last day the Phillies occupied first place in 1963. By May 11, they had sunk to ninth place in the ten-team National League. Take heart though—they rallied. By mid-July, our heroes had battled back to .500. They remained on the plus side of .500 for the remainder of the campaign.

By season's end, Mauch's charges boasted an 87–75 record, good for a fourth-place finish. Baldschun had chipped in 11 wins along with a sparkling 2.30 ERA.

CHAPTER 7

PUTSY CABALLERO

"What was the game of my life?" asks Putsy Caballero. "I think every Whiz Kid would give you the same answer. It had to be that game against the Dodgers—the last game of the year. We beat them in their own ballpark and won the National League pennant. That was our greatest thrill. That was my greatest thrill."

MEET PUTSY CABALLERO

"People ask me how I got the name 'Putsy,'" Ralph Joseph Caballero chirps. "I'll tell you, I really don't know where that name came from. As far back as I can remember, that's what I've been called. In New Orleans, everybody had a nickname. My brothers all have nicknames—like my brother Raymond is Rainbow and Monroe is Money.

"Maybe I can't tell you where my nickname comes from, but I can tell you a couple funny stories about it. When I first came up, those Philly announcers like Gene Kelly and By Saam got to calling me 'Putz' instead of 'Putsy.' Well, those two fellas call me over one day and show me a big stack of fan mail. Fans were writing letters to them complaining that 'Putz' has a whole different thing in Yiddish! 'Putz' was the kind of word they shouldn't have been saying on the air and the fans were offended. The thing was, the announcers didn't know what 'putz' meant and neither did I at the time. Anyway, they stopped

43

saying 'Putz' and started calling me 'Putsy' like they should have been calling me all along.

"Another thing about my name, Caballero, is a Spanish word that means 'gentleman.' My heritage is Spanish. A lot of fans thought I was Italian. There was a restaurant owner in Philly named Sam Framo who was Italian, and I used to eat at his restaurant all the time—for free. He never charged me 'cause he thought I was Italian. I never told him anything different. I just enjoyed the free food.

"I signed a contract with the Phils in '44. I was only 16 years old at the time. My father had to drive me up to Philadelphia to sign it. I was too young to sign it myself. Did you know I was the youngest player ever to play third base in the majors? Joe Nuxhall (who was born on July 28, 1930) the Cincinnati pitcher was the youngest player ever to appear in a major league game. Nuxhall was a bit younger than me when he made his first big league appearance. He was one month and 20 days short of his 16th birthday in his June 10, 1944 debut. But I'm the youngest third baseman ever."

Caballero was one month and 22 days short of his 17th birthday in his September 14, 1944 debut. A strange contrast between these two "childhood stars" is that Putsy was on the Phillies roster for the next eight seasons, which in the franchise's history is the fifth longest continuous major-league career spent entirely as a Philadelphia Phillie. Putsy retired in 1952, just as Joe Nuxhall was *resuming* his career. After 1944, Nuxhall did not resurface on the Cincy roster until 1952. The big lefthander went on to pitch for 15 consecutive seasons before hanging up the spikes in 1966 with a 135–117 career record.

"I've spent practically my whole life in New Orleans," continued Caballero. "But I loved my time in Philly. I roomed with Richie Ashburn who was a great guy. I named my oldest son, who was born in Philadelphia, after Richie. I remember the name of the doctor who delivered my son was Robertson. I was in St. Louis at the time. Richie Ashburn and a few of the other guys on the team took me out to celebrate. You see, back then it wasn't like it is today. Back then, no team would ever let a player go home for any reason, including having a baby.

Putsy Caballero played his entire eight-year major league career as a Phillie. Only four others had longer careers entirely as Phillies. *Photo by Brace Photography*

"After I quit the Phils, I worked in pest control. Two of my co-workers were Pete Fountain and Al Hirt. Can you believe that? My father-in-law owned a night club called Dan's International on Bourbon Street for years. I introduced Al and Pete to him. That's how they got their start in music. Once my father-in-law heard them play he said, 'Quit that roach job!' They quit but I stayed in that business for another 36 years.

"I'm still active. I still talk to Robin Roberts and some of the Whiz Kids once in a while. I'm just recovering from that Hurricane. I lost everything in Katrina, including my baseball memorabilia. I had some valuable stuff too. In Clearwater at spring training in 1948, Babe Ruth stopped by. I was awestruck to meet him. The Babe gave me a baseball that he signed. That was one of the things I lost. I think my memorabilia was valued at about $80,000 or $90,000.

"I still see photos of me as a Phillie. People tell me there's one popular picture floating around on the Internet. It's a photo of Jackie Robinson getting tagged out at third base. Jackie's sliding in and I'm the third baseman. Jackie, the Phillies, the Dodgers, the Whiz Kids—what great memories."

SETTING THE STAGE

"We were fighting and clawing to win Philly a pennant," says Caballero. "It all came down to the last game of the year up in Brooklyn. If we won, we won the pennant. If we lost, we were tied with the Dodgers and we'd have to play a one-game playoff to see who won the pennant. I think everybody wrote us off at that point because the Dodgers had come from pretty far behind to catch up to us. But we believed in ourselves and we went into that game confident we were going to win."

THE GAME OF MY LIFE
OCTOBER 1, 1950
BY PUTSY CABALLERO

Well I remember a lot about that game but I might get some of the details wrong. The image that's most vivid in my mind was that great play in the ninth inning when Richie Ashburn threw Cal Abrams out at the plate. Cal Abrams was one of the fastest guys around, but Richie made such a great play he got him. Ashburn was off and running at the sound of the bat. He got a better jump on the ball than anyone I ever saw and it really paid off on that play. Abrams was out by a long shot. I think every Phillie knew we were going to win after that play.

I got into that game too—it wasn't very spectacular. I wasn't a starter so I was sent in to pinch run. I tried to steal but Campy (Dodger catcher Roy Campanella) threw me out. That was the end of my day.

The other thing I can still see was that long, high fly that Pee Wee Reese hit off Robbie (Robin Roberts). The ball stayed up in the air so long and finally came down in the chicken wire in the fence—that tied the game. Then Richie's throw came later, but what a game and what a thrill it was to win a pennant.

WRAPPING IT UP

"Mr. Carpenter (owner of the Phils) asked us if we wanted to celebrate winning the pennant in Brooklyn or back in Philly," remembers Caballero. "We were staying at the Commodore Hotel in Brooklyn. I think the Commodore was at 42nd and Lexington. None of us wanted to celebrate up there in Brooklyn. We said, 'No, let's celebrate in Philly.'"

"After that 1950 season," he continues. "I only played two more years. I scouted for the Phillies for three years after I retired, but my main job since I left baseball was doing pest control. After doing it for 35 years, I retired ten years ago. I still root for the Phillies. I hope they win it again. It's been awhile now, hasn't it?"

CHAPTER 8

DON CARMAN

"If you're asking for my most memorable moment, that would be my first game," says Don Carman. "My first appearance came on October 1, 1983."

Carman pitched one perfect inning of relief to register a save for the '83 NL pennant-winning 'Wheeze Kids,' who already had the division wrapped up.

"But as for my most memorable game, I'd have to say there is one game that stands out above all the others," continues Carman. "That's my one-hitter against the Giants, but I have more reasons to remember that game than just the fact that it was a one-hitter."

MEET DON CARMAN

Donald Wayne Carman was one of the more reliable hurlers ever to don a Phillies uniform.

"Donnie had the kind of stuff that, when he was on, made him pretty unhittable," John Vukovich once said.

Anchoring the other half of a formidable Philly duo of lefties, Carman *was* virtually unhittable on a number of occasions. Twice, he limited the opposition to a single hit. If you think that's pedestrian, consider this: In the sum total of Phillies history of 124 years, only ten hurlers tossed multiple one-hitters, giving up one hit or fewer in a nine-inning game). The hurlers on that list comprise Phillie royalty: Grover Cleveland Alexander, Steve Carlton, Robin Roberts, Rick Wise, Jim Bunning, Russ Meyer, and finally, Don Carman.

"That other one-hitter I threw, the one against the Mets was different than the one I threw against the Giants," Carman muses. "I didn't make a bad pitch until the bottom of the ninth. Against the Mets, I made maybe 40 bad pitches or so, but I got away with them that particular day. One of those bad pitches was to Mookie Wilson. I put a pitch up and out over the plate to Mookie in the fourth inning and he didn't miss it—that's baseball."

In addition to those two impressive one-hitters, Don also registered a three-hit complete-game shutout over the Padres in '87 and a four-hit complete-game shutout against the Pirates in '86. As Vukovich said, Carman could be unhittable when he had his stuff. That means unhittable even to the guys who could really hit. Over his lifetime, he held the following illustrious group to a collective .025 average: Craig Biggio, Ken Griffey Jr. Jeff Leonard, Pete Rose, Larry Walker, and Matt Williams.

Returning to Carman's statement above, "That's baseball"—a statement he delivers with tongue planted in cheek. Carman made a splash during his playing days with a gentle poke of fun at the facile, clichéd non-answer that permeates interviews throughout the world of sport. As the baseball season grinds through 162 arduous summer days, enthusiasm for postgame discussions with the press wanes. Carman posted a list of 37 standard responses to annoying recurring clichéd questions, like "How'd you feel out there today, Don?" Response, "I didn't have my good stuff but I battled them," or "It's better to be lucky than good." He attached the list to his locker with instructions to reporters: "You saw the game. Take what you need."

Carman's name made Philly headlines in recent years for an off-the-field matter.

"I found a box of fan mail I hadn't answered," says Carman. "There were maybe 200, 250 letters. But they were about 15 years old. My whole career, I tried to answer every letter I received—I still do. I had brought this particular box along with us when we moved to Naples, Florida in 1991. I figured I'd answer the letters while I was relaxing, watching a football game. It didn't happen. My wife asked me to clean the garage years later—that's when I found the long-lost box of fan mail."

Don Carman is one of only 10 Phillies hurlers to toss more than one one-hitter.
Photo by Brace Photography

Better late than never, he personally answered every letter in the box that time had forgotten.

"Actually, it was lots of fun," he confesses. "I paid my 8-year-old son Jackson four dollars to open and sort the letters. Then, the two of us sat down together and looked through them. Jackson is too young ever to have seen me pitch, so he was really impressed by the flattering things he read. I got kind of swept up in the spirit, realizing these kids were now adults, so I started writing notes to them instead of just signing them.

"The funny part was taking them to the Naples Post Office. Can you imagine asking the teller for 250 ten-cent stamps and 250 four-cent stamps? The guy didn't know what was going on, but we stamped and sent them. I really loved the fans in Philly. It gave me real pleasure to finally answer those letters."

Ever the gentleman, Carman may have toyed a bit with the heads of the sportswriters on occasion but not the fans.

SETTING THE STAGE

Going into that game, I had been pitching poorly. Actually, they sent me to the bullpen and I was pitching poorly out there too. In an unusual move, to try to get me out of my slump, they brought me back into the starting rotation. It sounds strange, doesn't it? The normal way to pitch out of slump is to go down to the bullpen.

Naturally, I was concerned with the way I was pitching. Would you believe I was up until 3 a.m. in my hotel room the night before the game, trying to straighten out my mechanics? I could *not* figure out what was wrong with my delivery, so I practiced in front of the mirror in my hotel room for hours. Finally, I figured, 'Look, just pitch the way you did in high school because it's getting late. You've got a game to pitch tomorrow.' I knew I needed the rest.

Fans aren't aware of how nervous practically every pitcher gets before a game. I was more nervous than usual this day. But as I threw, I started feeling better and better. As a pitcher, when you're warming up before the game, you know right away if you've got your good stuff that day. While I was warming up, Claude Osteen was standing behind me watching. Ron Reynolds was catching me—he caught me in the game too. When we were walking back to the dugout from the pen, Ron started to say, 'You really got it today, Don.' But he never got the words out. Claude stopped him. You know, Bob, anyone who understands anything about baseball realizes you never say anything when a guy is on a roll. It kind of breaks the rhythm.

But I was going into the game in great shape, feeling good, but worried about that crazy unpredictable Candlestick Park weather.

THE GAME OF MY LIFE
AUGUST 16, 1986
BY DON CARMAN

This was only my second day back in the rotation. My thought process on the mound that day was great. I put everything exactly where I wanted it. I'd say to myself that I wanted to toss it two inches outside and that's just where the ball would wind up. Then I'd say, "Let's go three inches outside," and I'd put it right where I wanted it. I'd try to bounce one and get them to chase. And I'd bounce it right at the plate where I wanted to.

Candlestick Park in San Francisco was cold that day. I think there were only about 5,000 people in the stands (attendance was 10,723), but there was a group of about 50 people behind our dugout that were yelling the whole game. They were enjoying the refreshments they were drinking, but as the innings rolled along they thought they had a chance to witness a perfect game—they actually started to root for me, I think.

I started the game extremely strong. I struck the first two guys out looking (Dan Gladden and Robby Thompson). The third guy grounded out. After that inning, I did something I never did before—or since. When I was walking back to the dugout, as I crossed the foul line I said out loud, 'These guys are done.'

I had a lot of strikeouts. (Carman set the Giants down one-two-three every inning. The first inning that Carman failed to register a strikeout was the fifth). Mike Krukow, who was a good friend of mine, was pitching a great game himself that day. We couldn't get anything going against Mike either.

At the bottom of the eighth with two outs, Candy Maldonado tried to bunt. I was throwing a perfect game and Maldonado tries to bunt—I was ticked! I thought it was disrespectful. Candy is actually a friend of mine. I said to him after the game, "What were you doing trying to bunt? It's not like you can run!"

I mean, here's this big lumbering guy who can't run well trying to break up a perfect game with a bunt. (Candy stole only 34 bases in a

15-year career) So I'm out on the mound thinking, "If I throw at him, I lose my perfect game."

So I decided to pitch him up and in and glare in at him. Since I had such great control that day, that's exactly what I did. I ended up striking him out. As the game wore on, my 'friends' behind the stands started yelling, "You've got a perfect game going!"

Like I said, the longer the game got, the louder they yelled. I came to bat in the top of the ninth. We had gotten a couple of runners on (Juan Samuel led off with a single. Sammy was on the move as Ron Reynolds grounded to short. Reynolds was tossed out as Sammy advanced to second. Steve Jeltz singled, which put Phils on the corners with one out when Carman stepped to the plate). While I was on deck, (manager) John Felske kept yelling, "Donnie" at me.

Felske was trying to yank me back and pinch hit for me. I stood there with my back to him the whole time as he shouted louder and louder, But I refused to be taken out of the game. I never even turned around and got my at-bat (Carman tapped the ball to the first baseman, who threw home and caught Sammie in a run-down. Sammie was tagged out and the inning ended when Gary Redus, the next batter, flew out to right).

We didn't score, but like I said, I never felt as good as I did that day—not before or since. I'd plan to throw two fast balls away and then bounce a breaking ball and every pitch I planned went exactly where I wanted it to go. I never even went three balls deep in a count until I gave up an intentional walk in the ninth. Bob Brenly had led off the ninth with a double. I remember exactly what I threw him that at-bat.

Brenly was getting older at that point in his career, but he was still dangerous. I started him off with a breaking ball that he bounced foul down the third-base line. Next, I threw a thigh-high fastball away and he hit it on the nose into left-center. Milt Thompson was in center that day and Gary Redus was in left. They were two of the fastest guys in the league and, you know, after the game they both said they felt they could have caught up to it—who knows?

I was backing up third-base on Brenly's hit. All I could think was, "You went from a perfect game to a loss with one pitch!"

Remember we were tied 0–0 in the bottom of the ninth. But as I crossed the foul line coming back to the mound, I thought, "I'm not going to lose this game and I'm staying in. They're going to try to yank me out and there is no way I'm going to let that happen."

Mike Schmidt came in to the mound and called the rest of the infield in. He said, "I don't care what play they call from the dugout. Here's what we're going to do. I'll field the bunt and throw to third."

He told Steve Jeltz to cover third—that's exactly what happened. Schmidty kind of hung back until the last second, then rushed in with the pitch, fielded the ball, spun and threw to Jeltz for the out at third (Next, Mike Krukow, whom the Giants allowed to bat, sacrificed the runner, José Uribe, to second. Then, Carman walked Dan Gladden the next batter). I got through the inning without giving up a run (Joel Youngblood pinch-hitting for Robby Thompson made the final out). In the tenth, Juan Samuel led off with a homer. Steve Bedrosian came in and put them down in their half of the tenth—we won 1–0."

WRAPPING IT UP

"We pitchers are a worrisome group," adds Carman. "I've just now reached the point in my life where I can sleep on my left side. That's how concerned pitchers are with keeping their arms uninjured. I know one pitcher, who will remain nameless, who used to put tacks on the pajama sleeve of his pitching arm. That way if he rolled over on his pitching arm during the night, he'd wake up immediately."

CHAPTER 9

JOHN CALLISON

"I hate picking the game I'm going to pick," says John Callison. "No one on our '64 team will ever forget the 10-game skid in 1964. Neither will anyone in Philly. They were the worst couple of weeks of my life, but we didn't lose those games for lack of effort or choking. We were all busting our butts to win. We just couldn't get it together. And in the midst of all those losses I had, well, maybe the best game of my life. So I guess I'll go with the game I hit three homers against the Braves as the game of my life.

"I had some other big games in my career," Callison explains. "I hit for the cycle (against the Pirates on June 7, 1963). And of course there was the 1964 All-Star game. That was the game of my life in the sense of being the game I'm most remembered for."

Callison is remembered for that game because he did what only Ted Williams and Stan Musial ever did up until then—hit an All-Star game walk-off home run.

"But I look on the game of my life as a game that I played for my own team," he continues. "And even though we suffered through that horrible crash, the Phillies were my team, not the '64 All-Star squad. I loved my Phillies teammates and as painful as '64 was, I wouldn't have traded that year for the world. I wouldn't have traded any of my years in Philly for the world. After I got here, I made Philly my home for the rest of my life. I have so many wonderful memories here—and yes, that game down the stretch against the Braves in '64 was one of them, even though I did it in a losing cause."

MEET JOHNNY CALLISON

In the words of Callison's teammate Clay Dalrymple, "There's no telling how good Johnny could have been if he were two inches taller and 15 pounds heavier. As it is, he was one heck of a ballplayer."

When Callison arrived in Philly in 1960, manager Gene Mauch anointed him as the main building block for the Phillies of the sixties. After Johnny was in the Quaker City for a few years, Mauch declared to the press corps that his star player's name was no longer "Johnny" but rather "John." The change was a declaration of Callison's maturity and leadership role. The name change caught on about as successfully as the Phillies forties-era attempt to change the team's nickname from Phillies to Blue Jays. The organization could call the team anything it wanted, but the fans continued calling them the Phillies. Likewise, Callison remained forever "Johnny."

Together with Tony Gonzalez and Dick Allen, Johnny formed a formidable triumvirate at the heart of the Phillies attack. As Art Mahaffey puts it, "Johnny was a real talent. We played in a great era. Think of those outfielders in those years: Aaron, Mays, Clemente, and Frank Robinson. They were some of the greatest players of any era. Johnny was just overshadowed."

That didn't stop Callison from making his mark. In the ill-fated 1964 campaign, he was runner-up to Cardinal Ken Boyer in the MVP balloting. Had the Phillies won the pennant, that 1–2 MVP finish would likely have been reversed. That year, Callison ranked third in the senior circuit in home runs (31) and fifth in runs batted in (104).

Defensively, he led the National League in outfield assists four consecutive times, and once in double plays, and he accomplished this feat in the heyday of Mays and Clemente. He ended his career among the top five Phillies in home runs (185) and triples (84).

Callison was signed directly out of high school. He surged out of the blocks in professional baseball. In 1957, he was assigned to the Class-C Bakersfield Bears of the California League. As a rookie, he batted .340 with 17 home runs and 31 stolen bases. The next season, he was promoted to the Triple-A Indianapolis Indians, where he led the American Association in home runs. The next season, he split time between the Chicago White Sox and its minor-league farm club

---

John Callison was the MVP of the 1964 NL All-Star team and runner-up as '64 NL MVP.
Photo by Brace Photography

in Indianapolis. In December the Sox traded Johnny to the Phillies for third baseman Gene Freese.

Callison settled in quickly in Philadelphia. He earned All-Star recognition three times (1962, 1964, 1965). After his almost-MVP year in 1964, he came back with a big year in '65, again topping 30 home runs and 100 RBIs while leading the NL with 16 triples, a career-high. Johnny reprised his three-homer performance that year when he went yard three times against the Cubs on June 6. In '66, Johnny was the NL leader in doubles. After that season, however, his production tailed off sharply. "I was in a lot of physical pain for the last several years of my career," Callison explained. "The game took its toll on my body."

Callison never again socked 20 homers in a season, nor did he ever knock in more than 65 runs as a Phillie. After 1969, he was shipped to the Cubbies. He enjoyed a minor resurgence in 1970 with the Cubs, as he slammed 19 round-trippers and knocked in 68. However, he slipped drastically the following season and was shipped off to the Yankees. He closed out his career as a Bronx Bomber on a less than noteworthy season.

Callison passed away on October 12, 2006. His name popped up in the news a short time later. When the Samuel Alito (Supreme Court Justice) hearings were raging on, he told the press that as a kid, he was a huge Johnny Callison fan.

SETTING THE STAGE

WARNING: Longtime Phillies fans beware—this may be painful.

The Phillies were rolling along in 1964. The NL's 1964 pantheon of future immortals included Clemente, Aaron, Mays, Matthews, Koufax, Spahn, Marichal, and Gibson (Note to literati: since immortal means having no beginning and no end, granting immortal status to any ball player is an oxymoron—nonetheless the term is accepted in baseball jargon). Absent from that pantheon were the names of any Philadelphia Phillies. Phillie staff ace Jim Bunning came close but he didn't enjoy the universal acclaim of that crowd.

Despite its lack of "immortals," something was brewing in the City of Brotherly Love. There was a new kid in town—a rookie third-base talent named Richie Allen, who subsequently insisted on being addressed as Dick Allen. Allen immediately showed flashes of brilliance with Herculean blasts (that Phillies old-timers still hail). Allen was joined by a cast of fine players, who were already in place—guys like John Callison, Tony Gonzalez, Wes Covington, and Cookie Rojas.

The Phillies were skippered by the youngest manager in baseball—Gene Mauch. At 38 years old he was leading his team into pennant contention—unfamiliar territory not only for him and his young charges but also for the city's fans. Three years prior to the '64 season, the Phillies had dropped 107 games, including a record-setting 23 losses in a row. The Phillies' franchise was competing in its 81st campaign. They had never won a World Series to that point.

However, on September 21, the Fightin' Phillies returned to the friendly confines of Connie Mack Stadium boasting a 6 ½-game lead. Only a dozen games remained. They were shoo-ins—Not.

The Phillies lost the opening game of a three-day series against the Reds. Mahaffey was on the mound. Chico Ruiz was on third, and all-time great Frank Robinson was at the plate. Ruiz stole home as Robinson watched. It was the game's only run. As revered Philly writer Ray Kelly wrote in his *Evening Bulletin* column, "It's one of those things that simply isn't done. Nobody tries to steal home with a slugging great like Frank Robinson at the plate. Not in the sixth inning of a scoreless game."

Cincinnati went on to win the next two. When the Reds left town, the Phillies still held a 3½-game lead over them. The Giants and Cards trailed the Phillies by five. Next the Braves came to town. Although at that point Milwaukee—yes, you younger fans, they were not from Atlanta back then—had been mathematically eliminated from the pennant race. They were still a first-division club with a frightening offense. Powered by Hank Aaron, Rico Carty, Lee Maye, Joe Torre, Eddie Matthews, and Felipe Alou, the Braves were a force for any pitching staff to reckon with.

Coming into Philly, the Braves had scored 727 runs—by far the most in the senior circuit. Their production eclipsed St. Louis' 658, the league's second highest total. The Phillies ranked a respectable third with 651. The Braves took the opener 5–3 as 20-year-old Wade Blasingame bested Phillies ace Jim Bunning.

The Phillies' lead in the standings stood at three over second-place Cincinnati. Meanwhile, St. Louis had crept up to a 3½-game deficit. The next day, the Braves and Phillies battled through 12 innings. The Braves emerged victorious. In the Big Apple, the Mets were rolling over for the Reds in both ends of a doubleheader. The doubleheader sweep brought Cincinnati to within 1½ games of the front-runners. St. Louis was 2½ off the pace.

In the next game, the Phillies jumped off to a 4–0 lead after two innings. The Braves whittled that advantage down to 4–2 after seven, then narrowed the gap to 4–3 on a Gus Triandos passed ball in the eighth. In the top of the ninth, everything unraveled. Aaron and Matthews each singled. An error loaded the bases. Rico Carty followed with a shot off Bobby Shantz that sailed over Tony Gonzalez's head for a base-clearing triple.

"I've been joking with Tony for years now," Shantz quips these days. "I thought he had a chance on that ball, but Tony always tells me, 'I would have had a chance if I had been sitting in the bleachers.'"

The Braves put up a three-spot in the top of the inning. Warren Spahn, in the twilight of a Hall of Fame career, came in to relieve and set the Phillies down one-two-three. After the loss, the Phillies clung to a half-game lead over the Reds who, once again, had beat up on the Mets. Our hometowners headed into the final game of the Braves series on Sunday knowing that a loss coupled with a Red win meant dropping out of first place for the first time since July. Philadelphia's leader, Callison went into the contest determined to take matters into his own hands trying to hoist his dazzled mates on his shoulders.

THE GAME OF MY LIFE
APRIL 8, 1992
BY JOHN CALLISON

I really don't think we were panicking with all those losses. We couldn't catch a break—like that passed ball the day before and the triple that Carty hit. With a little less air under it, who knows? I do know that I went into that breakaway game thinking I needed to do something extra to win. We were going up against Tony Cloninger, who was tough. We were starting Jim Bunning on only three days' rest.

The game didn't start well. Felipe Alou led off with a single. I could almost hear the crowd grumbling, "Here we go again!" Then their second batter, Lee Maye, who had five hits on the day, doubled. Aaron was up next and he doubled. We were in the hole 2–0 before the Braves made an out. But we got out of the inning without further damage. In our half of the first, Tony Gonzalez led off with a double.

Richie Allen drove him in with a single and I came up and struck out. That strikeout was one of the low points of my career. I had a pitch or two to hit and I came up short. I do think I was pressing, trying to do too much. We got one run back and we were still in the game.

As I remember, Bunning set them down in order in the second inning. We had confidence when Bunning was on the hill. He worked himself into a game, like all the great pitchers do. If you didn't get him early, you were in for a long day. So when he mowed them down in the second, we thought we were in for a typical Bunning day—we weren't. I think Jim was just low on gas that day. He never quite found his rhythm. We came back in our half of the inning and went ahead by one. That was as good as it was going to get for us that day.

In the fourth, the Braves broke the game open. They knocked Bunning out. Dallas Green came in (as a pitcher, not a manager) and they knocked Dallas around. When the smoke cleared that inning, we were trailing 8–3. Then the bottom really fell out. The Braves scored more in the next two innings, and we found ourselves on the wrong end of a 12–3 score.

We were shell-shocked. But believe me, we didn't give in. We were determined to come back and we actually felt we could. I led off the sixth. I knew I had to do something big. I was swinging for the downs. Usually that doesn't work. In fact, it usually fails miserably. But it *did* work that day. I hit a home run. I opened up the eighth trying the same thing and I hit another one out. I hit that second homer off a guy named Chi-Chi Olivo. It didn't cut the lead much. We were still down big, but none of us had ever played in a game with so much at stake. Everything we had worked for all year long was going down the drain. So I think my homer lifted the team and showed everybody the game wasn't over.

The next time I came up, we had two outs in the bottom of the ninth. Practically everyone had left the park (the crowd was 20,569 that day). The fans that were left were booing like hell. I was determined again not to make the last out for the sake of pride and for the sake of not giving in and showing some character. Allen had doubled before me. There were two guys on and I got a pitch I could turn on—I got all of it. That brought us up to 14–6. I do think the fans appreciated my personal effort. They gave me a sincere good round of applause when I circled the bases. Unfortunately, Wes (Covington) struck out after me and the game was over.

I gave it all I had that day. I always did, but that day, I tried to hit the long ball and it worked. We went into the clubhouse knowing what was happening in New York. The Reds had won the first game of their doubleheader with the Mets. We found out shortly afterward that the Reds won the second game too. That put Cincinnati a full game ahead of us. And as everyone in this city knows, that was all she wrote for us. Maybe that's the story of my life—the best day of my career turned out to be the worst day of my life.

WRAPPING IT UP

Callison was at his best that day. As the day underscored, sometimes your best is not enough. He went only 12 for 48 during the ten-game losing skid. That doesn't qualify as the complete meltdown that many of his teammates experienced, but it was not Callison's finest hour.

By virtue of their 14–6 defeat, the Phillies had dropped seven games in seven days. Their meltdown tumbled them into second place. Philadelphia was in shock—arguably it still is. The Phillies evacuated the Quaker City and flew to St. Louis. Incredibly, they lost three more in succession to consecrate baseball's most infamous ten-game losing streak. Their abysmal demise was the worst ever for a first-place team so close to the season finale. But what Philadelphia baseball fan doesn't know *that*? However, all Philadelphia wants to thank New York for its 2007 meltdown. And how sweet it is that the Phils are the team that bested them.

Philadelphia left St. Louis 2 ½ games behind the now-first-place Cardinals. After feasting on the inept Mets, the Reds came down to earth as the Pirates beat them two out of three. The Reds returned to Philly and lost two straight to the Phillies. The Reds and Phillies finished tied for second, one game behind St. Louis. Interestingly, the Reds who initiated the Phillies' tumble on September 21 were coached by Dick Sisler who, a decade and a half earlier, had hit the biggest home run in Phillies history to win a pennant. Meanwhile, the guy on the mound on Sisler's big day, Robin Roberts, also won two games for the Baltimore Orioles as the Phillies' 10-game swoon rolled along.

Since the A's dynasty of the early thirties, nothing—not even the 1960 Eagles' magical season—had energized the city more than the Phillies' season-long-minus-12-game run. The collapse still fuels hot-stove league disputes. Many claimed that Mauch mishandled his starting pitchers. Some cite dissension as the culprit for the collapse. Others insist that the Ruiz steal burst the team's tenuous bubble.

Ruiz, who in Phillies lore takes as much heat as Joe Carter for killing the dreams of Phillies fans, is an intriguing story post-1964. As Paul Harvey would say, here's the rest of the story on Chico.

Chico stole only two bases over the next two seasons. He never hit another home run. He played in the major leagues for eight years. His batting average was a mediocre .240, but he did make the evening news on two occasions subsequent to his fabled steal of home. On the first occasion, he allegedly threatened a teammate at gunpoint in a 1971 clubhouse incident. The second occasion was when he died at the young age of 33 in a 1972 car accident. Ruiz is probably more famous in Philadelphia than in his Cuban hometown.

CHAPTER 10

CHRIS WHEELER

"Give me a few days to think about this one," says Chris Wheeler. "I live and die with the Phils and I've watched them play so many heart-thumpers over the years. I've also seen so many milestones like Carlton's 3,000th strikeout, Schmidt's 500th home run, and several Pete Rose games. I've got a definite game in mind, but let me think them all over and I'll get back to you in a few days."

A few days later . . . .

"Okay Bob, one particular game does stick out, although you've probably heard about this game from some of the other guys you've talked to in your book. Still it's the biggest, most exciting game I ever saw.

"The game was the final episode of what had to be one of the greatest baseball postseason series ever played—I mean that too. It was one of the most hotly contested, hard-fought series ever—and I say that for more reasons than just my love of the Phillies. For one thing, back then, there were no Wild Card and League Championship Series were five-game affairs. That put more pressure on teams to win every game. With no Wild Card, you had to win your Division to make it into postseason play and anything and everything could, and sometimes did, happen in that short five-game series. Well this was the series where everything did happen and I was fortunate enough to be in the booth to witness it all unfold. I'm talking, of course, about the 1980 National League Championship Series. It all came down to the fifth and final game—and that game is the game of my life."

MEET CHRIS WHEELER

Chris Wheeler was born on August 9, 1945, in Philadelphia. On that particular Thursday, the Phillies dropped a 3–1 decision to the Pirates, which sank their won-lost record to 27–75, .265, 38 ½ games behind en route to a 46–108 season. Fortunately, it's been mostly uphill for the Phillies ever since—at least that's the way Chris Wheeler seems to view things. Wheeler is a lifelong Phillie fanatic.

As his friend Tom Burgoyne, the "best friend" of the Phillie Phanatic, puts it, "Wheels just loves baseball. He is baseball's equivalent of the gym rat in basketball. His whole life, Wheels could never get enough baseball."

When he was young, Wheeler's family moved from Yeadon to Newtown Square within Pennsylvania where he spent his summers on the ball fields.

"I lived and breathed baseball when I grew up," Wheeler explains. "My dad took us to Connie Mack Stadium for Phillies games every chance we got. As I got older, I made the trip myself. I'd take the bus to 69th Street then hop the Phillies Express to the subway at Lehigh Avenue. I'd have gone to the ends of the earth to catch a Phillies game."

Wheeler played infield for Marple Newtown High and realized that he didn't have the requisite skills to make baseball his career. He pursued his major-league dreams via an alternative path. Chris majored in journalism and broadcasting at Penn State where he hosted a radio show with Joe Paterno in '66. After graduation, he flooded the Philly market with resumes and eventually landed a job with Philly's WCAU radio. He left WCAU—first, for a stint at WBBM in the Windy City, and later, for a position at CBS radio in the Big Apple. However, he was a Philly boy who always yearned to return to his native city.

In 1971, when the Phillies were seeking help in their PR department, they solicited some names of candidates for the position from Andy Musser, a WCAU sportscaster at the time. Musser recommended Wheeler.

"My first day with the Phils was on July 5, 1971," remembers Wheeler when they bested Atlanta 6–5, behind Woody Fryman. "I was going to be working for the team I loved. I thought I had gone

---

Chris Wheeler, or "Wheels," has been on the Phillies broadcast team since 1977.

to heaven. I couldn't wait to start my job. Then, when I reported to work my first day, things got even better. My first assignment was to drive some of the 'Hot Pants Girls' to a promotion at Dilworth Plaza in Center City. I did—even though it was tough duty for a 25-year-old. When I got back to the Vet later that afternoon, (Manager) Frank Lucchesi showed me around the clubhouse. Then we sat down and talked baseball for over an hour. All I could think was, '*This* is exactly what I wanted my whole life.'

"In 1976, the Phils clinched the NL East title in Montreal in the first game of a doubleheader (September 25). Harry (Kalas) and Whitey (Ashburn) had to leave the booth to go down to the locker room to do the postgame interviews with the champagne corks flying and everything. We were short of people in the booth (Robin Roberts and Andy Musser were the others on the broadcasting team in that bicentennial year), so I got to fill in. I was on cloud nine. The next year, I became part of the official broadcast team and I've been part of it ever since. This year (2007) marks my 31st season in the booth.

"It's funny how things work out. When I was a kid, I had a friend named Ed Pappas. Ed and I used to play across the street from Bill Campbell's house and impersonate Bill calling a Phillies game. We were hoping Bill would give us a job. Little did I know that one day I would end up calling the Phils games—just like Bill Campbell."

SETTING THE STAGE

"I'll run through the first four games of that incredible 1980 NLCS briefly," says Chris Wheeler. "The Phillies won the first game. I think the schedule helped them out. To advance to the NLCS, the Astros had to win a playoff game with the Dodgers for the Western Division Championship. Immediately after the Dodger game, they flew from Houston all the way across the country to Philadelphia. I think that gave the Phillies a huge advantage. The Astros *had* to be tired. Most fans don't realize how grueling a 162-game schedule is with the constant travel—packing and unpacking. Of course, baseball's a funny game and you can't predict what's going to happen.

"Game one turned out to be normal. 'Lefty' (Steve Carlton) battled Bob Forsch for a 3–1 win. The Bull basically decided the game with a two-run home run in the sixth that put us up by one. Greg Gross—one of the great clutch hitters I've ever seen—added an insurance run in the seventh and that was all we needed. Tug came in for the save at the end. Little did we know that this game—a typical Lefty-type game—would set the stage for the 'bizarre-ness' of the rest of the series.

"We went on to lose game two, which turned out to be the first edition in a sequence of four successive extra-inning games. We should have won game two in the ninth but a bizarre base-running mix-up at third prevented us from scoring and we went down in extra innings. Then it was off to Houston. I felt that the pressure was on the Phillies because of all the disappointments in postseason play over the preceding few years. Remember, the Phillies made the postseason playoff in '76, '77, and '78, and in each of those years they failed to advance to the World Series. This year, however, I think there was added pressure. Philly fans felt that the opponent this year wasn't up to the caliber of the opponents that defeated the Phillies in the '76, '77, and '78 National League Championship Series. We weren't going up against a super team, like the 'Big Red Machine' or the Dodgers with Garvey, our current coach Dave Lopes, Ron Cey, and all those great pitchers. We were *only* playing the Astros.

"Game three was the second straight extra-inning game. The contest was decided in the 11th on a sacrifice fly by the Astros' Denny Walling that scored Rafael Landestoy from third. Landestoy was pinch-running for Joe Morgan, who had led off the inning with a triple. Tug McGraw pitched three innings in that game. No wonder he was dead by the end of the World Series. After the game, I was sitting in the bus and John Vukovich walked in and sat down beside me. Vuke and I were best of friends even back then. I was stepping on my lip at the time, feeling sorry for myself because we were about to go down again in the postseason and I just couldn't bear the thought. Another loss meant another winter of banquets and answering fans' questions about why we failed again. Vuke told me to get my head up. He insisted that we were not only going to win the next two games— we were going to win the World Series too. I didn't believe what he was saying then and I still don't, but he was right.

"The Saturday game was nuts. You can chronicle it as it careened into extra innings with the bizarre 'triple play that wasn't' (the triple play was ruled a DP), with the Astros' tying the score in the ninth, and with Pete Rose running over catcher Bruce Bochy with the winning run in the tenth. Pete scored on a Luzinski pinch-double. Pete should have been out by 30 feet but he bowled Bochy over and scored the winning run. And then Tug went out and pitched another inning.

So here comes game number five on a Sunday night at the frenzied Astrodome. I had never heard noise like I heard in that place and I haven't since.

THE GAME OF MY LIFE
OCTOBER 12, 1980
BY CHRIS WHEELER

The pitching matchup wasn't so hot for us that day. The great Nolan Ryan was going up against rookie RHP Marty Bystrom, who had done a fabulous job in September in helping us make it into post-season play. But this matchup didn't look so good on paper. The game was close. We were tied 2–2 after six innings, but the fun was just ready to begin. Of course, that was the way the whole series went.

In the Astros half of the seventh, they put up a three-spot off Larry Christensen and Ron Reed and the Dome went nuts. I'll be honest. I thought it was all over for us and I guess that's the way almost everyone else felt—everyone else except that remarkable bunch of 1980 Phillies players. Seriously, how good are your chances when you're three runs down with Nolan Ryan on the mound and you only have six outs left in the game? Not only that, the Astros had Dave Smith waiting in the bullpen. Wow, what a pitching staff that club had, to say the least. In the seventh inning, we were not in a very enviable position. We were certainly in no position to start thinking about a trip to the World Series.

I still marvel at what happened next. Within two minutes, the Phillies had the bases loaded with nobody out and the Dome crowd got a little quieter and was starting to squirm. Still, you had to think, there was no way Ryan was going to lose a three-run lead. After all, this guy was one of the greatest pitchers of all time. But, as every Philadelphia fan knows, Ryan did lose that lead. Manny Trillo capped the five-run eighth by hitting a triple down the left-field line—that put us two up. But in that wacky series, that wasn't enough. The Astros came right back and scored two off a dead-tired Tug McGraw to tie the game at seven. There was no scoring in the ninth so the game went into the tenth inning, which meant we were playing the fourth straight extra-inning game.

I was in the booth and never felt so drained. I couldn't imagine what those guys on the field were feeling. Later, I found out they felt better than we did broadcasting the game. Greg Luzinski told me after the game that he looked up at the press box and saw me with my head on the microphone in the radio booth and he started laughing. He said he realized that he and his Phillie mates had the power to do something about what was happening. But all we could do up in that press box was watch.

In the tenth inning, we got a huge two-out double to right from Del Unser. Then Garry Maddox, the Secretary of Defense, doubled to center to score a go-ahead run. Dick Ruthven came in and closed the door in the bottom of the inning. I can still hear myself whooping and hollering as Andy Musser called the final out. That final out—the fly ball off the bat of Enos Cabell settling into Garry Maddox' glove—remains one of the most vivid images I have in all my years of cheering on the Phillies.

That moment—that celebration in the booth as the final act was recorded—was probably not the most professional moment of my career, but it certainly was the most spontaneous. The LCS was over and we finally came out on top. We had an amazing clubhouse celebration that continued when we got back to the Shamrock Hilton Hotel in Houston. Then we got a few hours sleep on a red-eye flight back to Philadelphia where we kicked off the first World Series in town in 30 years. The World Series was great—as was the result. So too was the unforgettable parade down Broad Street. But among all those incredible memories, the game I'll never forget—the game I remember most in my 36 years with the Phillies is that electric night in Houston when a bunch of men just wouldn't give in on losing their dream of playing in the World Series. We all went along on their amazing ride—and it was spectacular.

WRAPPING IT UP

After the Phillies' great victory on Columbus Day in 1980, they went on to win their first and only World Series championship. In fact, it was the Phillies' only postseason Columbus Day victory in four October 12 contests.

CHAPTER 11

MAJE McDONNELL

"How do I pick one game out of the past 60 years?" asks Maje McDonnell. "Actually I can. I'll never forget the game where we won the 1950 pennant over the Dodgers—that was the finest moment ever."

MEET MAJE McDONNELL

Robert A. "Maje" McDonnell was tagged with the nickname "Maje" early on.

"I was always dribbling a basketball or tossing a baseball," he recalls. "Somebody said I was like a 'real major leaguer.' So I went from 'Major League' to 'Major' to 'Maje.' I've been Maje longer than I can remember."

Maje graduated from Northeast High School in 1938 where he played both baseball and basketball. After his days at Northeast, he attended Brown Prep at 15th and Race for a year.

"Max Patkin, the old 'Clown Prince of Baseball' was one of my classmates," Maje emphasizes. After that I became the first guy from St. Anne's Parish in Port Richmond who ever got a scholarship to Villanova. They gave it to me for basketball at first—then they switched it to half-baseball/ half-basketball. By splitting up the scholarship that way, both the baseball and basketball program had more money for scholarships than if one of them had given me the whole thing.

While Maje was pitching for the Villanova Wildcats, he took the mound in an exhibition contest against the Philadelphia Phillies. He lost the game 7–6, but former Yankee great Herb Pennock, who was with the Phillies' front office in the late forties, was impressed by Maje's performance.

"I threw strikes," Maje points out. "Herb said he'd work with me on increasing my velocity and teaching me another pitch cause he thought I could compete at a major-league level, even though I didn't have major-league size.

"My only appearance as a Phillie was in an exhibition game against Waterbury Connecticut, "Maje explains. "I pitched six scoreless innings in '47. I pitched three more scoreless innings in '48 and a few more for Wilmington. They were going to put me on the roster in '51 but it didn't happen. There was some kid in the minors that the Phillies were going to lose if they didn't bring him up, so that took my opportunity away—but you know, I was still happy. While I was working for the Phillies during that period, I was coaching at Villanova. I was an assistant coach for the varsity, but I was the coach of the freshman teams."

McDonnell's freshman teams fashioned a 117–18 record under his tutelage. One of his squads went a perfect 22–0.

"Larry Hennessey was on that one," Maje continues. "He was the big Wildcat star after Paul Arizin left."

Maje believes he might be the only man who ever coached in both a World Series and an NCAA tournament (actually four NCAA tournaments). Trivia buffs can chew on that one for its veracity.

Maje became a Phillie scout in 1958, scouring western Pennsylvania for talent. Ballantine Beer wooed Maje away from the Phils. Fans of "a certain age" might recall Three-Ring Pete and other Ballantine bytes that supplied the soundtrack for Philly summers in the fifties. While Maje was a Ballantine employee, he coached at Chestnut Hill Academy.

"Bill Giles came over to see me one day," Maje goes on. "He told me, 'You belong with the Phillies, Maje. You're a Phillie. Come back with us and we'll find a place for you.' I did. I came back to the Phils. I've been with them ever since."

Maje and his wife, Mildred Mary, have been married for 60 years. They have three daughters, only one of whom has departed the Quaker City area.

Maje McDonnell sports a perfect ERA in Phillies' exhibition games, but never appeared in a regular-season contest. *Photo by Brace Photography*

"I was born and raised in Philly and never wanted to be anyplace else," Maje trumpets. "I'm just a Philly guy."

SETTING THE STAGE

The Phillies were going great guns in 1950. The Carpenter program of signing bonus babies was bearing fruit. Curt Simmons was a sensation. Robin Roberts had found his Hall of Fame groove as had center fielder, Richie Ashburn. Del Ennis had blossomed into one of the game's premier sluggers. Jim Konstanty, the bespectacled, professorial-looking, palmball-flinging relief pitcher who had been brought over from the Boston Braves was enjoying an MVP season. Granny Hamner, Puddin' Head Jones, and Andy Seminick were becoming fan favorites. The Phillies were the darlings of Philly—as proof, for the first time since 1915, they led the Senior Circuit in attendance.

They had a 7½-game lead as late as September 17 with only 13 games to play. Twelve games later, on Saturday, September 30 that lead had dwindled down to one game when the Dodgers topped the Phillies 7–3 at Ebbets Field. There was only one game left to play in the season. In the season finale on October 1, Philadelphia was squaring up against Brooklyn, the team that trailed them by a single game. A loss would cause a Brooklyn-Philadelphia tie for the pennant.

Unfortunately for the Phillies, as history would eventually prove, the Whiz Kids were contemporaneous with another embryonic juggernaut that was to outplay and overshadow them. Brooklyn's legendary, poetically homaged Boys of Summer team had a date with destiny.

"It was tough at the end of the year," Maje recalls. "Brooklyn kept closing the gap between us (starting on September 19, Brooklyn won eight straight games). Curt Simmons was lost to military service. I never saw Curt throw better than he did that year. I still think we'd have won the whole thing if Curt had played the whole season and had been allowed to pitch in the World Series."

The loss of Simmons wasn't the only blow the Whiz Kids' pitching staff had to withstand. Bob Miller hurt himself carrying a suitcase at the 30th Street Station. Miller had started the '50 campaign 8–0. He was never the same after that freak injury. He ended the '50 season with an impressive 11–6 record. However, as the Phils roared or crawled to the finish line, Miller could only chip in with a 3–6 record—not the stuff of pennant winners. Bubba Church, another guy who had done a yeoman job on the mound, was also hurt after being whacked by a line drive off the bat of Ted Kluszewski. Suddenly at the end of the year, the high-flying young Whiz Kids found themselves holding on for dear life, in grave danger of becoming the 'Fizz Kids.'

On October 1, the Phillies walked into Ebbets Field in a must-win, no-tomorrow situation (actually there would have been a tomorrow in the form of a single-game playoff against the red hot Dodgers—naturally that was not viewed as a desirable outcome of the season finale). The Phillies sent their young ace, Robin Roberts, to the mound. The Dodgers countered with Don Newcombe—their ace.

THE GAME OF MY LIFE
OCTOBER 1, 1950
BY MAJE McDONNELL

The game was a typical Roberts-Newcombe match. Runs were hard to come by. It was a real hot day–that was a benefit. Robbie always seemed to be tougher when the weather was hot. The temperature that momentous afternoon soared to 88.4 degrees at 3:45 p.m., a record high for the date up to that point. (The previous record of 88.3 for October 1 was recorded in 1881).

We were up 1–0 in the sixth. That's when little Pee Wee Reese hit a long ball to right that lodged in the screen on the right-field wall. I don't think it was a home run, but that's what the umpire called it. And the Dodgers tied the game—just like that. That's the way the game stayed until the ninth.

We failed to score in the top of the ninth. Cal Abrams, the Dodgers' lead-off batter drew a walk. I think Robbie walked Abrams twice on the day. The count was 3–2 to Abrams and he took a close pitch that was called a ball. It looked like a strike to us. So the Dodgers put the winning run on base right off the bat. Then Pee Wee Reese tried to bunt a couple of pitches and missed. So what did he do? He lined one to center for a single. Abrams stopped at second and then the Dodgers had Duke Snider up. Duke lined the first pitch to center for a hit. But Richie Ashburn, who was as fine a centerfielder as I've ever seen, came in fast and scooped up the ball.

Richie rifled it to Stan Lopata at the plate and Abrams was out by a mile. I still think the Dodger third-base coach, Milt Stock, did the right thing sending Abrams. Against anyone else, Abrams would have made it safe. It's just that Richie made such a great play.

But even then, the Dodgers had men on second and third with Jackie Robinson coming up. You didn't get a break in that Dodger lineup. Our Robbie walked their Robbie intentionally to fill the bases. Then Carl Furillo popped up to Eddie Waitkus at first base and the next batter, Gil Hodges, hit a long fly to Del Ennis in right-center near the scoreboard.

So it was our turn again. And don't you know, Robbie comes up and lines a single. You could feel the momentum swing. We just knew we were going to get them. Waitkus made one bunt attempt and failed. Then he singled into center. Richie Ashburn came up next and tried to bunt Robbie to third, but Newk (Brooklyn pitcher Don Newcombe) made a great play and forced Robbie at third. That brought Dick Sisler to the plate. Dick already had three singles that day, but he nailed this one to left. It was a short fence out there but Dick got enough of the ball for it to sail out. Sisler's three-run homer put us up 4–1.

In the Dodger half of the tenth, Robbie set the Dodgers down in order, starting with Roy Campanella—so the game ended 4–1. I can remember that game like it was yesterday. And I remember the feeling—how great we all felt. And I never saw anything like what awaited us back in Philly. We took the train down to 30th Street Station and it looked like a million people were there waiting for us.

WRAPPING IT UP

The *New York Times* reported the Phillies-Dodgers game in their October 2, 1950 edition stating, "The Philadelphia Whiz Kids, who came so close to winning the ignominious title of the Fizz Kids, captured the first National League pennant for the Quaker City in thirty-five years when they beat the Dodgers, 4–1, yesterday at Ebbets Field before the greatest outpouring of Flatbush fans (35,073) of the 1950 season."

"Robbie was really on that day," Maje concludes. "He was either striking the Dodgers out or getting them to hit the ball on the ground. Roberts only gave up five or six hits."

Robbie himself was credited with six assists and a putout. First baseman Eddie Waitkus registered 17 putouts. Robbie surrendered five hits with Pee Wee Reese accounting for three of them.

With their big win over the Brooks, the Phillies ended their 1950 campaign the same way they had started it—with Robin Roberts besting Don Newcombe at Ebbets Field. With his season-finale victory, Roberts recorded his 20th win. In the process, he became the first Phillies' 20-game winner since 1917, when Grover Cleveland Alexander turned in his third consecutive 30-win season. Roberts had failed in his six previous 1950 starts to nail down number 20.

CHAPTER 12

DEL UNSER

"I've been thinking about my answer for a while," says Del Unser, when asked for the game of his life. "I come up with three different games. I guess you're going to make me pick only one though, aren't you?

"Well, it's tough not to pick my first big-league at-bat. I don't think any major-leaguer ever forgets that. It's the culmination of a lifelong dream, something that you've worked for all your life. I made an out. I hit a one-hopper. I really got good wood on it. But it went right to Bert Campaneris (shortstop) and I was out. It was still a thrill to hit it hard up here in the big leagues and gain a little confidence. Of course, I wasn't a Phillie that game, so that disqualifies that choice.

"The second game that comes to my mind is the fifth game of the Houston League Championship Series," he continues. "I pinch hit in the eighth inning and got a single off Bob Forsch—that kept the inning going and we scored three more. Later in the game (the tenth), I doubled for another big hit (each following a Mike Schmidt whiff). Garry Maddox doubled me in for the winning run in the NLCS. Now, there's a thrill a ball player doesn't forget. That series was the most important I've ever played—that's for sure. And I think anyone, any baseball fan, has to admit, it was one of the most exciting series ever played. I was thrilled to be part of it all. It was history really.

"The third game—this is the game I'll pick as *the* game. I set a pinch-hitting record in this game when I hit my third straight, pinch-hit home run."

MEET DEL UNSER

Del Unser grew up in Decatur, Illinois. His baseball talents led him to Mississippi State University. You may not be aware of the school's baseball tradition, but MSU has produced some impressive major league baseball players. In addition to Del, the school's alumni roster boasts the likes of Will Clark, Alex Grammas, Buddy Myer, Rafael Palmeiro, Jeff Brantley, and Bobby Thigpen.

Unser was drafted three times before he finally signed a major league contract. In 1965, the Twins chose him in the second round. In 1966, the Pirates took him in the fourth round. Finally in '66, the Washington Senators made him their first-round (18th overall) choice and Unser signed. Two years later, he was their starting center fielder. He broke in with an unimpressive .230 rookie batting average. However, he did lead the hapless Senators in a few categories such as at-bats, stolen bases, and singles. Furthermore, he was chosen *The Sporting News* AL Rookie of the Year. Unser was a skilled outfielder, who rated defensively below only Paul Blair. Unser led all AL outfielders in assists, double plays, and total chances per game while finishing second in putouts.

The following season, Unser had a breakout year. Although Frank Howard, who was at the peak of his career, led the Senators in virtually every offensive category, Unser managed to garner some attention. He led the AL in triples, although by doing so he set the record for hitting the fewest triples ever to lead the league. He posted a five-hit game (four singles and a round-tripper) against the A's. He also had a four-hit game. In that contest, he slapped a single, two doubles and a homer to drive in four and score two. For his efforts, he placed 23rd in the AL, MVP voting that year (Harmon Killebrew was the winner).

Unser was dealt to the Cleveland Indians, where he spent the 1972 season, before packing his bags for Philadelphia, in exchange for Oscar Gamble and Roger Freed. He started for the '73 and '74 Phillies and led the team in batting average his first season in the Quaker City. Unser also discovered some batting power—slamming 11 homers. He had averaged fewer than five homers per season in his previous five campaigns. One of his 11 homers was a three-run blast

---

Del Unser tied the major league mark when he hit his third consecutive pinch-hit home run off Hall of Famer Rollie Fingers. *Photo by Brace Photography*

on June 26, 1973 off Hall-of-Fame-bound, Bob Gibson. He drove in four that day. Interestingly, Unser had tremendous success against Gibson, as well as Gibson's contemporaries destined for the Hall of Fame, Ferguson Jenkins and Nolan Ryan. His career average against that formidable trio was .432 (16 for 37).

The following season, Unser matched his 11 round-trippers of the previous season. Although his batting average tailed off to a .264, he put up career highs for RBIs (61) and runs (72). After the season, he was a major player in a blockbuster deal. Unser, Mac Scarce, and John Stearns were all sent to the Mets for Tug McGraw, Don Hahn, and Dave Schneck. Unser's inaugural season for the Mets turned out to be the acme of his pro career. He batted .294 to top all his teammates and also slammed ten homers. Despite that production, the following season he was given a ticket to Montreal. There, for the first time in his career, he was relegated to the status of spot starter—a role he would play until the end of his career. He was granted free agency by Montreal on November 2, 1978.

"I was in a racquetball tournament in Las Vegas," Unser recalls. "Paul Owens called me and asked me what I was doing. I told him I was playing racquetball and he growled something about, 'Why don't you come here and play baseball?' I rushed back to California, where we were living and headed to Philly. I signed on and played the next four years in Philadelphia. They were great years. The 1980 season was the highlight of my career."

Unser came to Philly and immediately shined in his pinch-hitter role. In '79, he batted .304 in the pinch and tied a ML record with homers in three straight pinch at-bats. He pinch hit .316 in 1980, when the Phillies won their one and only World Championship. In the decisive game five of the LCS, he went two-for-two, first delivering a pinch hit and then remaining in the game to drive in a run and score the game-winning run in the tenth inning.

In Game 2 of the World Series, he hit a pinch double off Royals relief ace Dan Quisenberry in the Phillies' eighth-inning come-from-behind rally. In Game Five, another pinch double off Quisenberry in the ninth inning tied the game; Unser moved to third on a sacrifice fly and scored the game winner on an infield single.

"We were really on a great roll that year," Unser grimaces. "We were the following year too. Then, the strike came and we never got our momentum back. I can't complain. It's partly our fault, but that was kind of the end of that team."

The following year, Unser called it quits. On June 6, in his final at-bat, he pinch-hit for pitcher Ed Farmer and flied out to center field.

"I was only out of the game a short while," he explains. "When I came back, I was a hitting instructor for the Phils for a while. I've maintained a good relationship with the Phils throughout my career. I started off traveling the minor league circuit with Granny Hamner—that's a book in itself. Besides being a great golfer and a terrific pool shooter, Granny was one of baseball's all-time characters. These days, I'm traveling constantly on special assignments doing things like checking out players the Phils might be interested in trading for. Pat (Gillick the GM) keeps me busy. I'm writing reports all the time in hotel rooms, but then afterward, I spend a lot of time on the phone with Pat. He puts a lot of work into the operation and demands that I do as well. Of course, I thrive on it and look forward to performing this role for several more years."

SETTING THE STAGE

Prior to the '79 season, the Phils had traded for Pete Rose. Charley Hustle was considered the missing ingredient that the talent-laden, underachieving Phillies of the late seventies needed to reach the elusive next level. With the addition of Rose, the Phillies themselves felt they were a sure bet to go all the way. They had won their division three consecutive seasons prior to '79. However, they slipped drastically in '79 when they won *only* 90 games—a total that was nonetheless sufficient to capture their division. Those 90 victories represented a decline of 11 in the win column from the 101 victories they compiled in both the '76 and '77 campaigns.

Entering the game on July 10, the Phillies were starting to pick up steam. They were in third place at 45–40, 5½ games off the pace-setting Expos. But the Fightins had strung three consecutive victories together. Nino Espinosa was on the hill for Philadelphia facing Randy Jones, whose glory years were behind him. He had been a feared 20-game winner in '74 and '75, but subsequent to those glory years was never to register another winning season.

In addition to the importance of the July 10 game, Unser was vying for a slot in major-league history. He had hit a pinch home run on June 30. He reprised that dinger in his next pinch hit appearance on July 5. His next pinch-hit outing would afford him the chance to tie the major-league record for most consecutive pinch-hit home runs. Lee Lacy had set the record a season earlier. There was a good crowd at the Vet for the rare afternoon contest. Unser was a fan favorite. All of Philly knew about his chance to make history.

THE GAME OF MY LIFE
JULY 10, 1979
BY DEL UNSER

I wasn't really much of a slugger. I was pretty successful as a pinch hitter, but I was never a power hitter. Still I was on a good roll around that time. I was seeing the ball real good. I think what I'm happiest about is that my home runs were key hits that often led to victories.

The first game of that three-game streak (June 30) was against the Cardinals in St. Louis. We went into the ninth inning down 4–1. But the Bull (Greg Luzinski) hit a homer with two out (Rose and Schmidt had each flied out). Garry Maddox followed with a single. Then I pinch hit for Manny Trillo, because they brought a right hander in (George Frazier who replaced John Fulgham) and I hit one to tie the game. The next batter, Dave Rader, grounded out, but my hit put the game into extra innings. Then in the top of the tenth we put a bunch of singles together, scored a couple, and won 6–4.

My second pinch-hit homer came against the Mets. I pinch hit in the seventh off Craig Swan. We were down 3–0 and not doing much. Boonie (catcher Bob Boone) got a lead-off single. Then we made a couple outs and I pinch hit for Larry Bowa and got a good pitch to hit. I drove in the only runs and Swan finished the game, which we lost 3–2.

The third pinch-hit homer, though, was the most gratifying. I hit it off a Hall of Famer, Rollie Fingers. Randy Jones started for the Padres that day and he was on his game. We were down by a run or so when the Padres had a big inning in the middle of the game (San Diego scored four in the fifth on back-to-back triples by Gene Richards and Ozzie Smith and a double by Fernando Gonzalez).

So we were down 5–1 and that's the way it stayed until the ninth. Randy Jones was still in there and the Vet fans were still cheering. They never give up. Garry Maddox opened the inning with a ground-out though, and things didn't look too promising, but then we got a couple of singles and they yanked Randy Jones. They brought in Rollie Fingers, who was really tough. Boonie got a hit and McCarver followed with a single. Bake McBride hit a grounder and his speed avoided a double play, which would have ended the game. Then I came up to pinch hit. There were two on and two out. We were down 5–3. A home run would give us a 6–5 win. Well, Rollie gave me one to hit and I got it all—the fans went wild. This was one of those records that you knew about. I mean, I knew when I hit the ball I had tied the record—that was terrific in itself. But to hit a walk-off home run off Rollie Fingers—well, that made the whole thing incredible."

WRAPPING IT UP

The Phillies fell to fourth place in 1979. On August 31, Dallas Green replaced Danny Ozark as the Phils' manager—a move that many credit for the team's success the following season. Unser contributed heftily to that championship season in 1980. After his heroics in the decisive game of the thrilling 1980 NLCS, he showed his knack for timely hitting again in the World Series.

The Phillies continued their come-from-behind groove when Kansas City headed to the Vet in Philly two days later. The Fightins spotted Kansas City four runs in three innings. But in the bottom of the third, the Phils roared ahead 5–4 on Bake McBride's three-run blast. To the delight of the Vet throng, the hometown fans went on to a 7–6 victory—their first World Series victory since October 8, 1915.

The following game, Unser repeated his eighth-inning NLCS heroics. With the Phillies trailing 4–2, he led off the inning with a double to light off a four-run spree and surge the Phillies to a 6–4 advantage. He stayed in the game, replacing Luzinski in left. Ron Reed came on in relief of Steve Carlton and preserved the victory.

In game five, Unser again played a crucial role. In the ninth inning, with the Phillies trailing 3–2, Del came to bat with no outs and Mike Schmidt on first. He doubled Schmidt in to knot the score at three. Manny Trillo's single plated Unser with what proved to be the winning run.

CHAPTER 13

KEVIN JORDAN

"The game of my life has to be my very first game with the Phils, August 8, 1995," says Kevin Jordan. "Most of the other games over the course of my career are tough to recall precisely. The details blur and blend together. I think, in general, ballplayers tend to remember particular at-bats, not particular games. Starting in AA ball, I kept a log of every at-bat I ever had until I retired. As for the games I remember most. . . . I'd say the first game I ever played in the majors has to be the game I remember most. Anytime you realize your life's dream, it's got to be a memorable day. I remember all the details of that day because it was so hectic, emotional, and exciting. Everything happened so fast that day. I had so many emotions running around inside me. So, yeah, my big-league debut—for a number of reasons, that's the game I'll always remember most."

MEET KEVIN JORDAN

"As early as I can remember, I wanted to be a professional ballplayer," Kevin Jordan confesses. "Even when I was in the minors, I couldn't get enough baseball. I used to play minor league games and rush home to watch *Baseball Tonight*. The whole time I was watching, I'd be thinking, 'I can't wait to get up there myself!'

"My dad has been my role model and friend. He helped me realize my dream. Even after I was playing professionally, he used to pitch batting practice to me. My dad refused to put a screen in front of him for protection. Even when I had fully grown and could hit the ball hard, he pitched with no protection. Early on, he saw that I had a God-given talent for baseball. My dad helped cultivate that. He'd have worked hard with me no matter what I showed an inclination for. If I had liked playing the guitar, he would have encouraged me in that—he was that kind of dad. He became my role model once I became a dad myself."

Jordan attended one of the most accomplished high schools in the country, Lowell High School in San Francisco. Lowell, a public magnet school, is the oldest public high school west of the Mississippi. Lowell was ranked as the #26 high school in the US in 2006 by *Newsweek*'s Jay Mathews Challenge Index. Kevin graduated from Lowell in 1987. He was drafted by the Dodgers in the tenth round of the 1989 amateur draft, but did not sign. He was attending the University of Nebraska at the time.

Then on June 4, 1990, the Yankees plucked him in the 20th round of the 1990 amateur draft. This time, Kevin inked a Yankee contract. He spent the next four seasons in the Yankee farm system. On February 9, 1994, Kevin was part of a blockbuster trade. The Yanks sent Ryan Karp and Bobby Munoz to the Phillies for Terry Mulholland and a player to be named later, who turned out to be Jeff Patterson.

Kevin hung around a couple of years in the Phillies' farm system before joining the parent club for a seven-year stint. He waited a few years after his 2001 retirement from active play to return to the game he loves. The Phillies signed him up as the hitting instructor for the Atlantic League. These days, he focuses his energy on helping young hopefuls on the Phillies Lakewood Blue Claws farm club achieve their own dreams.

SETTING THE STAGE

"I was in Scranton kind of hoping or expecting I might get called up to the Phils," says Jordan. "I grabbed the *USA Today* this particular day—August 8, 1995. It was about one o'clock in the afternoon. I was in my apartment. We had a game that evening, so I was just hanging around waiting to go to the park at about two or two-thirty. There was a little blurb in the sports section on baseball

When Kevin Jordan reported to Philadelphia, he left his girlfriend locked in the car. "I heard it was a dangerous city," he said. *David Seelig/Getty Images*

transactions. Cincinnati had picked up Mariano Duncan from the Phillies on waivers. With Mariano leaving Philadelphia, I thought, I hoped, it would create a roster opening for an infielder. At that point in my career, I felt I had a good shot at getting the call. At the same time, nobody had to tell me that nothing in this game is automatic.

"The phone rang shortly afterward. It was our manager. He asked me to come to his office right away. I had a feeling the Duncan deal had something to do with the call, but he didn't say. I didn't ask. So I headed in to see him right away. He congratulated me and told me I had to drive down to Philadelphia right away to join the team. They had a home game that night. That's when the fun started."

THE GAME OF MY LIFE
AUGUST 8, 1995
BY KEVIN JORDAN

As soon as he told me I was going to the big time, the day got crazy. I had to say goodbye to my teammates—as many as I could find. They were just starting to drift into the clubhouse. But I didn't have much time to linger. I had to go back to my apartment to pack. I left the Scranton clubhouse quickly and headed back. Nina's from Papua, New Guinea. She had only been in the U.S. for about two weeks. Fortunately, she hadn't been here long enough to look for work. If she had been working, I would have had more problems to deal with. We packed up everything we had in our Honda Accord and headed down to Philly. Before we left, I called my dad up and told him I was going to the majors. He was so proud and happy. That was another thing that made my day.

I followed the directions they gave me from Scranton to Philly. We had to fight our way through rush-hour traffic. I think we got lost trying to find the Stadium. I didn't know this area at all. I was filled with all kinds of excitement and emotion. I hardly knew anybody on the Phillies team. When we finally got to the Vet, I pulled into the parking lot. The attendant welcomed me; he is still with the Phillies. He's a great guy. He didn't know who I was so he directed me to the media parking lot. I didn't know anything about the city of Philadelphia. The only thing I heard about Philly was that it was a dangerous city. I told Nina, who's now my wife, to wait in the car. I didn't think she'd be safe if she got out. Even though it was a hot, muggy, August Philly day, she stayed in the car with the windows up and the motor running.

I went into the Vet. I didn't know where to go, or where I was supposed to go. They directed me to Frank Copenbarger, the clubhouse guy who's been with the Phillies for so long. Frank walked me over to my locker. It used to be Dave Cash's locker. That was exciting in itself. As I said, I grew up a huge baseball fan. I watched all the major league games I could. Dave Cash was a star—a guy I particularly admired since he was an infielder. Now here I was all of a sudden using the same locker he had.

Fans don't realize it but ballplayers kind of get into their own routines or zones in a clubhouse. Each guy prepares for a game in his own way. When I walked into the clubhouse, our batting practice was over. The guys were mentally preparing for the game. So I felt like I was on an island. It might sound funny to fans, but there's nothing in our lives that prepares ballplayers for what I call the "circus of baseball."

The game on the diamond doesn't change. We're prepared for that—at least I was. My whole life had been baseball. But the rest of the circus—the media, the bright lights, the huge stadium, the noise, the TV cameras—there's no preparation for that. I remember walking out onto that field at the Vet for the first time. The place seemed colossal, huge, and intimidating. Sure, I had played in some other big stadiums, but nothing like the Vet. I don't know why it looks so large from the field—but it does. Maybe it's because the Vet wasn't built as a baseball stadium. It went up as one of those all-purpose stadiums that were so popular in the seventies. The perspective from the Vet dugout, which was below the field level, kind of made everything appear bigger and more spectacular.

Another thing that probably sounds strange to the fans is—well basically, I didn't know where I was allowed to go. I was in the clubhouse, but I didn't know anybody, and wasn't comfortable going anywhere. I didn't know what rooms were off-limits. There were lots of rooms downstairs in the Vet, but I didn't dare leave the clubhouse. Eventually it was time to head out to the field. I sat on the bench with Tony Longmire, Jim Eisenreich, and Dave Gallagher. I had met those guys in the Grapefruit League so I just followed their lead. About the fourth inning, they asked me to go back to the video room. At that point in every game, the guys on the bench headed back to stretch and hit off a batting tee and generally loosen up. I was supposed to limber up "in case I got the call."

It dawned on me at that point that being a pinch hitter was totally new to me. That's got to be a strange feeling for every guy who gets called up to the majors. Up to that point in any player's career, he was a starter. I hadn't pinch hit much, if ever. All through high school, college and the minors, I had been a starter.

Sure enough, in the ninth inning, John Vukovich, who was the bench coach called my name and told me to grab a bat. We went into the inning behind 12–6. I stepped out into the batting circle which, at the Vet, was kind of close to the stands. I could hear the buzz and no one had any idea who I was. I did everything the same way I always did. I had the doughnut on my bat, but you know Bob, I don't think I could really feel my body. It was such a strange experience. I had so many emotions floating around my head. It was trying to drink in that circus atmosphere. The game between the lines was the same, but the rest of the scene was completely different. Everything was on such a gigantic scale—the TV coverage, the huge stadium, the noise level.

Mark Whiten opened the ninth with a single. Then Dutch Daulton hit his second homer of the day and the Vet was rocking. Lucky for me, the pitcher was Dave Telgheder, a guy I had faced before. The first pitch he threw me was a fast ball right down the middle and I took it. The next pitch, I pulled one down the left-field line that hooked foul. The third pitch, I lined to center. The Mets' centerfielder Damon Buford raced in, slid and caught the ball. When I hit the ball, I thought I had myself a hit. The trouble was I hit it a little too well. The ball hung up and Buford caught up to it. I hit it just a little too far. The umpire, Cowboy Joe West, called me out.

When I got back to the dugout, our guys were all encouraging me, "Good hit. You got robbed." I'll never forget Curt Schilling. He came running down to me and said, "He trapped that ball! They robbed you of a hit!" It made me feel good that a star like Schilling was paying attention to me. Schilling was always good to me. We've remained good friends to this day.

We almost came back that inning. After my line-out, Kevin Stocker singled, Charley Hayes walked, and we got a couple more but fell a couple short. The game ended 12–10. It was an exciting comeback—just not enough.

Once the game ended, I realized I hadn't thought of anything but baseball from the moment I arrived that afternoon. When the game was over, suddenly the rest of the "stuff" hit me like, "What happened to my girlfriend?!" The last time I saw her she was sitting in the car with the motor running and the windows up! I found out after the game that they had brought her into the park but not until she had sat outside for about 45 minutes!

A bunch of other practical matters suddenly hit me, like, "Where were we going to sleep that night?" When I arrived, the Phillies told me they had gotten us a room. They put us up in the Holiday Inn near the Stadium. Unfortunately, the Holiday Inn didn't have any regular rooms left. They had to put us up in a business suite that didn't have any beds, only furniture. We put sofa cushions on the floor and slept on them.

That's how I ended the most exciting and hectic day of my life.

WRAPPING IT UP

Two days later, Jordan got his first start but took the collar in five at-bats. A week later, he smacked out his first hit.

"I hit it off Greg Swindell," he recounts. "I had watched him in the College World Series on TV and then in the pros and here I was on the same field with him batting against him. That's a thrill I'll always appreciate. I was on the same field with guys like Robby Thompson, who was coaching. I watched Robby play when I was growing up in San Francisco—same thing with Mark McGuire. I remember when he was trying to break in as a third baseman for the A's. All of a sudden, I was on the same field with him. The best part was that I felt I belonged. That's what drove me. I never lost the appreciation of how fortunate I was to be part of professional baseball. I played every game like it was my last.

"I never considered myself 'special' because I was a baseball player," he continued. "I always thought it was more important to be a good son and a good parent. Baseball was a bonus. It was simply my good fortune to have enough natural talent to play.

"It was a privilege to play major league baseball though. I remember walking up the runway with my son. We were headed out to the field for a Father/Son day at the Vet. My son's name is Kevin too. The fans saw me coming. They were all yelling, 'Kevin!' My little boy thought they were yelling for him and I thought, 'Wow, we really *are* fortunate.' When I was a kid, I saw the Giant players with their kids and I remember thinking how lucky those kids were. Now my own son was the lucky one.

"These days I'm teaching other young men what I learned—it's funny," explains Jordan. "I never realized how much I was learning those seven years I spent as a major leaguer. I find I have a lot of knowledge to impart and I want to share it to help other young people experience the exhilaration I was so fortunate to enjoy."

Incidentally, Kevin and Nina stayed at the Holiday Inn three days. Then for the rest of 1995, they moved into an apartment abandoned by someone who had been traded from the Phillies. The best part of the aftermath is that Kevin discovered that Philadelphia isn't such a scary place after all. Though he and Nina own a home in Australia, which they visit frequently, they make this their permanent home in the City of Brotherly Love.

CHAPTER 14

DANNY LITWHILER

"Wow, it was a long time ago that I played in Philly," says Danny Litwhiler. "I started my major league career there, you know. I played a few seasons then moved on to St. Louis, Boston, and Cincinnati. I spent my whole career—all 11 years—in the National League. I guess you better tell your readers that Boston had a team in the National League in my heyday. I played with the Boston Braves of the National League years before they moved to Milwaukee. Of course, most readers won't even remember the Milwaukee Braves. They only know them as the Atlanta Braves.

"As for the game I remember most in Philly, that's hard to say. We didn't have many big games when I was there. We weren't such a good team. But I do remember one game when I almost spoiled the season for the Dodgers. I guess that's a game that I never forgot, even though that game was played—let's see—how many years ago? . . . I guess it was 66 years ago. Wow that's something."

MEET DAN LITWHILER

Daniel Webster Litwhiler remains spry and alert, 65 years after he turned the page on a successful baseball career. The former right-handed throwing and hitting outfield star finished his 11-season career with a .281 batting average, 451 RBIs, and 107 home runs. He was the Phillies All-Star rep in 1942. Litwhiler didn't start in the Classic—that's no shame. He had to vie for a starting spot with a few Hall of Famers: Mel Ott, Joe "Ducky" Medwick, and Enos Slaughter.

"I grew up in a rural place called Ringtown in western Pennsylvania," Litwhiler relates. "I wound up at Bloomsburg State Teacher's College. I played ball there a few years. There were 14 state teachers colleges in Pennsylvania back then. We played in our own league. Actually, I played professional ball at the same time I was playing college ball. Yeah, I know—that doesn't sound right, but there was some rule back then—don't ask me what it was exactly, cause I can't remember—that allowed players in that particular state college league to play major-league ball while they were still in college. So, when I was a junior, I was signed by the Detroit Tigers. But I was injured and I didn't play because of the injury. I had a bad knee, but I went back and played another year at Bloomsburg. Then the Phillies signed me and I went to Philadelphia.

"I started playing with the Phils in 1940 but I wasn't a starter. I was honored to have played with Chuck Klein. Chuck started in right field when I first got to the Phils. Of course, Chuck was at the end of his career when I got there. But Chuck was my idol as a kid and he kind of took me under his wing and stood up for me when I arrived. Rookies had to take a lot of abuse in those days and not just from the regulars. The managers were tough too.

"I remember one game when I was in right field when Chuck was no longer starting. A ball was hit out to me and I threw it into Nick Etten, our first baseman. I had a good shot at getting the guy out since the runner made too big a turn around first. Well Nick didn't see what the runner did. The runner knew he couldn't make it back to first, so he figured he might as well try for second, even though he didn't have a chance to make it. But Nick didn't see the guy head toward second. If he had seen him, Nick could have thrown to second and beaten the runner by several feet. But as I said, Nick didn't and the guy ended up on second. When I got into the dugout after the inning was over, our manager Doc Prothro started screaming at me, yelling that I threw the ball behind the runner. Chuck Klein ran over and defended me. He said I made the right play. Chuck gave me a lot of confidence and made me feel I belonged."

Litwhiler gained enough confidence to earn a berth on the 1942 All-Star squad. The Phillies had a pathetic squad that year that finished last with a 42–109 record. Litwhiler led the squad in virtually

Dan Litwhiler was the Phillies' sole representative on the 1942 All-Star team.
Photo by Brace Photography

every offensive category: batting average, home runs (with nine, which makes that 42–109 record more understandable), doubles, triples, and runs scored. He also became the first Phillie regular at any position to record a perfect 1.000 Fielding Percentage for the season. Nonetheless, in what Connie Mack had made a great Philadelphia tradition, Litwhiler was shipped out after his All-Star season. In the early phase of the 1943 season, he was off to St. Louis. For his part, he lucked out. He landed a starting slot on the NL pennant-winning St. Louis Cardinals. There he teamed with the legendary Stan "The Man" Musial and Harry "The Hat" Walker in the Redbird outfield.

Litwhiler didn't have a memorable '44 World Series. Neither did the Cardinals, who dropped two of three at Yankee Stadium before losing their fourth at St. Louis' Sportsmans Park. In game number three, he chipped in with two singles in a losing cause (he had taken the collar in the first two contests). Incidentally Nick Etten, his old first-base friend from the Phillies was the starting first sacker for the Yankees in the Series.

"It was a thrill getting to play in the World Series," Litwhiler reflects.

He slammed 15 homers (the most in his career) the following year for the defending Cardinals. That total was second best on St. Louis, and surpassed Stan the Man's round-tripper production by three. Danny also knocked in 82 runs—fourth best on the team. This time, in a rare non-New York "Subway Series," the Cardinals emerged as World Champs, besting their AL neighbors, the St. Louis Browns (destined to become the Baltimore Orioles a decade hence), four games to two. Litwhiler was a big star in the Cardinal's 2–0 victory in game number five. His eighth-inning solo blast gave the Cardinals some breathing room in a hard-fought pitching match between Mort Cooper and Denny Galehouse.

In June the following season, he was sold to the Boston Braves—a team on the upswing. For the first time, he was not a starter. The Braves finished fourth that season. They climbed to third in 1947. Then in 1948, they won the NL pennant. However, Danny wasn't there for the champagne. The Braves dealt him to Cincinnati in May. The Reds were assuredly not a team on the rise. They finished in the seventh spot, immediately below the Phillies. Litwhiler still didn't start, but he did see considerable action. He slammed 14 homers in 338 at-bats—third best on the squad. In '49, though Danny was again a spot player, he put up impressive stats. In 292 at-bats, he batted .291 with 11 homers.

Litwhiler played three more seasons as a spot player before retiring from active play in 1951.

"They were wonderful years, my years in baseball," he reminisces. "A few years ago, they asked me to do a book on my years in baseball. I wrote it by hand and sent it to a guy who typed it all out and then they published it. It's called *Living the Baseball Dream.* I wasn't happy because they priced it too high. It was selling for almost 45 dollars and I thought it should be less than 30 dollars, but a lot of great stories are in it. And I tell them the way they happened."

SETTING THE STAGE

"We weren't going anywhere," says Litwhiler. "It was the end of another bad year for the Phils. But you know, if you're not going to win a pennant yourself, one of the big thrills in baseball is to play the spoiler role. Guys take lots of pride in showing opponents that are in the pennant race that they can still play this game. So, when we were playing the Dodgers at the end of the '42 season, the Dodgers still had a chance to win the pennant, as I recall. Their final two games were against us in Philadelphia."

THE GAME OF MY LIFE
SEPTEMBER 27, 1942
BY DANNY LITWHILER

We were playing our home games in Shibe Park in those days. My brother lived in southern Jersey. He and his wife tried to get up to see me every chance they got. They came up to this game, but there was a big crowd because the Brooklyn people all came down to see the game. My brother got there late and had to park a good distance from the stadium. There was no parking lot at Shibe Park. You had to park your car on the street. The neighborhood kids would come up to you when you got out of your car and say, "I'll watch your car for a quarter, Mister." Then you had to give them a quarter or they'd soap your car.

Well somehow—and I can't exactly remember how—the Dodgers had a chance to win the pennant if they won this final game against us. (*Editor's note: The situation was as follows: St. Louis led the Dodgers by two. The Cards' Saturday game against the Cubs was rained out, and they were playing a doubleheader to end the season. If the Dodgers beat the Phils and the Cards lost both games of the twin bill, the NL pennant would end in a Dodgers-Cards stalemate*). So we had a kind of big game. The Dodgers scored first but then we tied (Future Hall of Famer Lloyd Waner drove in catcher Tommy Livingston). The Dodgers went ahead, and then in the sixth, we got two men on and I came to bat. The Dodgers had Kirby Higby on the mound. I hit a long blast into right center. Here's the funny part. My brother and sister-in-law had just made it into the park at that point. She went to the ladies room and heard this tremendous roar. She ran out and asked the first guy she saw what had happened. The guy was a Brooklyn fan and he said to her, 'Some SOB from the Phillies just took the pennant away from us!' That SOB turned out to be me. I hit that ball real good and two men scored. But I tried to stretch it into a triple and I was thrown out.

Anyway, that was all we scored. We were down 4–3 after my double and the game ended that way. But as it turned out, the Dodgers didn't win the pennant after all. St. Louis won the first game of their doubleheader and it was all over. But at least I gave those Dodgers a scare."

WRAPPING IT UP

The Dodgers lost the pennant anyway, as Litwhiler points out. They gave two consecutive thumpings to the Phils at Shibe Park on the final two days of the regular season. They had won their final eight straight regular-season games, but their late run couldn't overcome the huge rush the Cards staged late in the season. The Dodgers had led the NL by 10 games as late as August 4, but the surging Cardinals overtook them. In all, Brooklyn won 104 games, which represented the highest total for a runner-up since 1909. To put that total in perspective, the most wins a Phillie team ever recorded was 101 (in '76 and '77), and our Phils accrued those totals in a 162-game season.

The *New York Times* the following day phrased the Dodgers demise eloquently: "Pennantville, viewed so admiringly and confidently as their certain destination by the Dodgers a little more than a month ago, today became only a dissolving mirage."

CHAPTER 15

DICKIE NOLES

"I know most people will think my answer is crazy," says Dickie Noles of his selection for the game of his life. "Having played in the World Series and in playoff games, I think most fans probably expect that I'd pick one of those big games—like when I gave George Brett a bowtie (i.e., pitched him high and tight). But the game I remember most is my first. I think every major-leaguer treasures his first game—I know I do. I always will. I was so happy and nervous at the same time—after all, that debut was about achieving my life's dream."

MEET DICKIE NOLES

Dickie Ray Noles has a story to tell.

"I've been working on a book for a few years now," says Noles. "I've sent a draft to the publishing house. The book's called *A Simple Life*."

In contrast to the Paris Hilton, Nicole Ritchie, brain-fried pabulum of the same title, Noles' opus is pithy.

"My mom was raped and that's how I was conceived," explains Noles. "She's the strongest person I know, the way she handled things and raised me. That's what my book is about."

Noles' personal story is absorbing too. He battled alcohol addiction for a number of dark years before he became straight and sober. Dickie is now the guy who deals with Human Resource issues in the Phillies' major- and minor-league operations. That makes him a man on the move, which is a role familiar to him from his active playing years.

Noles came up with the Phillies in their disappointing 1979 season. After getting acclimated, he became a vital cog on the pitching staff the following season—the championship year of 1980. He scratched his name into World Series lore in the '80 World Series against the Kansas City Royals. The marquee player for each of the combatants was a third baseman, Mike Schmidt for the Phillies and George Brett for the Royals. The Phils were a bit lethargic after a tense NLCS with Houston. They called on Noles to fire them up by loosening up Brett. He was never one to duck a challenge or a fight. Noles buzzed a pitch by the future Hall of Famer. His bowtie re-energized his mates, who went on to dispatch the Royals and claim their only World Series championship.

With the glory of the championship season behind, Dickie found himself ticketed for Chicago. He made 30 starts and pitched 170 innings for the fifth-place Cubs in 1982. Both were high-water marks for his career. Again in 1983, while his ex-mates in Philly were winning an NL pennant, he was toiling for the fifth-place Cubbies. Ex-mate Dick Ruthven reunited with him on the Chicago staff in mid-season and went 12–9, for the best winning percentage among Cub hurlers.

On July 2, 1984, Dickie packed his bags for Texas, which led to a baseball oddity that few others (and perhaps no other) in the long history of the game can claim. His ERA was exactly the same for both teams. He had a 5.15 ERA both for the Cubs, where he pitched 50 ⅔ innings and for Texas where he hurled 57⅔ innings.

Noles hurled 110⅔ innings for the Rangers in 1985—the last time his innings pitched total would attain triple figures. After the season, the Rangers released him and he was signed as a free agent by the Cleveland Indians. The rest of his career was spent in Chicago, Cleveland, Detroit, and Baltimore before he finally came home to roost in the Quaker City for his final season.

Dickie battled demons during his career—a battle that unquestionably diminished his statistics and performance. He prevailed in those battles against the bottle and now shares his experience and wisdom with players in the Phillies system. Noles is a popular figure and speaker around the Philly area.

Dickie Noles was popular as a pitcher with the Phils. These days he does human resource work for the organization. *Focus on Sport/Getty Images*

SETTING THE STAGE

"My build-up to the game was my entire lifetime of preparation and dreaming about being a big-league ballplayer," says Noles. "I never wanted to do anything else but be a baseball player. When I was in high school, I was the best hitter on the team. I was wild and so they didn't pitch me too often. But the main reason I played the outfield was that I wanted to play every day. When the manager brought me in to pitch, I think he was scared I'd hit every batter I faced, but I fooled him—I didn't hit anyone. Then the Phils ended up drafting me as a pitcher-outfielder. The Phils were the ones who decided I was going to be a pitcher. I wouldn't have cared. I just wanted to make it to the big leagues any way I could. So the road I took was as a pitcher.

"After I was drafted, I played three and a half years in the minors," he continued. "Finally they brought me up the day after Fourth of July. I was so excited. I didn't know anyone in the clubhouse—well hardly anyone. I think the only guys I knew were Warren Brusstar and Kevin Saucier. Otherwise, I was a stranger in that clubhouse.

"I didn't sleep a wink the night before I pitched. I was staying at the Hilton. I think it's a Howard Johnson's now. I stayed up all night. I was too excited to sleep. I mean, the Phillies—they were my team when I was in high school. That's when I started following them. They had Mike Schmidt and, like I said, I was as much a hitter as pitcher in high school, so Schmidty was my hero—same for Pete Rose. What kid wouldn't be star struck to walk into a major-league clubhouse and realize that he was a teammate of Pete Rose?

"So here I was, an unknown kid walking into a clubhouse with all these big stars—and *I* was going to pitch. Sure, I couldn't sleep, but I managed to get to the park and I've never been so excited in my life."

THE GAME OF MY LIFE
JULY 5, 1979
BY DICKIE NOLES

I didn't start out too well. Joel Youngblood led off the game with a homer. I don't think that shook me up too bad. The stands looked real crowded to me. I wasn't used to playing in front of that many people (attendance at Veterans Stadium that day was 28,720). But I think I was pretty much in control. After that home run, I settled down. They got another hit in the first inning, but no other scores.

The Phils weren't playing up to expectations when I came up. I think they were over .500 (the Phils were 42–39 at that point), but it was Pete Rose's first year, and the expectations were high. The Phillie fans weren't real happy.

I started to pitch myself into the game in the second inning. Unfortunately we didn't score. I was pitching against Craig Swan, who was 7–6 going into the contest. He finished the season 14–13. Although Swan's record is not very impressive, Swan was the ace of the NY staff that year. No other Met pitcher won even half as many games as Swan that season.

I got my first at-bat in the second inning. I struck out trying to bunt a couple of runners up. We loaded the bases—I think Manny Trillo walked after me, but we didn't score After the Trillo walk, Larry Bowa popped up to end the inning.

In the third, I got my first strikeout in the majors—It was Craig Swan. A couple of batters later, I struck out Frank Taveras.

In the fourth, the Mets scored a couple more. I know Richie Hebner had a double, and I think Willie Montanez drove a run in. Willie drove in Lee Mazzilli, who opened the inning with a walk. Later John Stearns drove Hebner in with a sacrifice fly. At the end of the inning, we were behind 3–0.

I only pitched one more inning. I set them down one-two-three with a couple of strikeouts—but that was it. In the sixth, Rawley Eastwick came in. Rawley and Kevin Saucier held the Mets the rest of the way, but our offense couldn't get anything going. In the seventh, Del Unser hit a two-run homer—but that was it. We fell one run short.

I wish the game of my life had a different ending—we lost. But I think at the end of the day I had proven to myself that I could pitch to major leaguers. That was all I ever dreamed of doing—making it to the big leagues and competing with the best players in the world. That was the dream of my life and it came true that day, even though I didn't win the game.

WRAPPING IT UP

Noles didn't have to wait long for his first victory. It came less than a week later at the expense of the San Francisco Giants. On July

9, 1979, he went up against Vida Blue. Though Noles threw only 65 strikes in 132 pitches and issued free passes to nine Giants, he allowed only two earned runs in 8 ⅓ innings. In the ninth, after getting one out, he walked two consecutive Giants. Warren Brusstar came on in relief and preserved Noles' 4–2 victory.

CHAPTER 16

KEVIN STOCKER

"I loved playing in Philly," says Kevin Stocker. "I played for a couple other major league teams, but I always consider the Phillies as my team and I never had as much fun playing ball as I did in 1993. As for the game of my life, it's a tough call. I'd still have to call my debut on July 7, 1993, the game of my life. It's the game I remember most. That 15–14 game in the World Series was amazing too. I never saw an individual battle like that World Series. The two teams battled but then there was the Lenny Dykstra and Paul Molitor battle too. Every time the Dude (Dykstra) did something good, Molitor would come back and match it. It was amazing to see. But still in all, the first game I ever played for the Phils, for a number of reasons, is the game of my life."

MEET KEVIN STOCKER

Kevin Douglas Stocker was born in Spokane Washington on February 13, 1970—that's *Friday*, February 13. But Kevin certainly was anything but a bad luck charm for the 1993 Phillies. He arrived in Philadelphia on July 7, 1993 when the Phillies were in desperate need of a quality fielding shortstop to stay atop the National League standings—a position they tenaciously retained from beginning to end of that charmed campaign.

As Jim Fregosi puts it, "When we brought Kevin up, we told him not to worry about hitting. The guy went out and hit, what, .324 or so? Without Stocker doing the job he did, we don't win that pennant that year.

"Here's the funny thing. All season long, Larry Bowa (who coached the '93 squad) is running up to me every day saying, 'Bring that kid Stocker up. We got to bring that kid Stocker up.' So one day after the Fourth of July I call Larry in to tell him Stocker's getting called up and he starts saying to me in that high-pitched voice he has, 'Do you think he can play at this level?'"

Stocker's path to the Phillies in 1993 started in the Spokane area and led him to the University of Washington where he starred from 1989 to '91. Twice, Kevin was selected to the all-Pacific-10 squad. The Phillies drafted Kevin in the second round of the 1991 amateur draft, inking him to a Phillies contract on June 3, 1991.

Stocker spent a couple of years in the Phillies minor league system before being called up to the Phillies on July 7, 1993. He had unparalleled success at the plate as a rookie. Fregosi didn't miss that figure. Stocker batted .324 for the pennant winners. In so doing, he set the single-season, high-water mark for batting average among all post-1900 Phillies shortstops. While Kevin never again approached such airy heights, he followed up with a respectable .270 in the strike-shortened '94 campaign.

In 1997, after batting .266 and belting 23 doubles, he was shipped to Tampa Bay in the 1997 expansion draft in exchange for Bobby Abreu. Kevin batted a horrible .208 in his first season for the Devil Rays. However, he redeemed himself the following year with a .299 average. On May 25, 2000, Tampa Bay released him after Kevin had appeared in 40 games. On May 30, the Anaheim Angels picked him up and Stocker finished out the season with the Halos. After the 2000 season, he called it quits.

After his playing days, Kevin hooked on with the College Sports Television Network (CSTV). How did Kevin Stocker land that gig?

"We were trying to establish a national voice for college baseball," explains Joel Feld, CSTV's executive vice president. "We had a list of guys we auditioned, because we want to find new, young, untapped talent. We want to develop our own guys. Kevin has never done anything like this, but there was something about him we liked."

"I love doing the color commentary," says Stocker by cell phone, en route to broadcasting a game in Alabama. "I love baseball and this job gives me a chance to stay involved in the game. I keep active. I'm

Kevin Stocker batted .324 as a 1993 Phillie. Manager Jim Fregosi says, "Without Stocker doing the job he did, we don't win the pennant." *Stephen Dunn/Getty Images*

managing to do some other things too. I run the Spokane Baseball Academy and I was managing the Spokane River Sharks until last year. My latest venture is opening three Emerald City Smoothie stores in the Spokane area—my wife and I are doing that. How did we get into it? Well, my wife is in excellent shape. She runs triathlons, so training and diet are very important to her. We each got interested in the Emerald City Smoothies because they're nutritional and healthy. They suffice as meals themselves. So for personal as well as business reasons, we're excited about the venture. Between announcing college games, volunteering for church service, and now running these three new stores, I'm extremely busy. But I will tell you that I miss Philly. I played for a couple of other major league teams besides Philadelphia, but to me, the Phillies will always be my team."

Kevin lives in Spokane with his wife, Brooke, and their three children, McKenna, Logan, and Zachary.

SETTING THE STAGE

The Phillies stampeded out of the gate in 1993. By the end of April, they were 17–5 with a 4 ½-game lead over second-place St. Louis. They cooled off a bit in May, posting a 17–10 log for the month. As May turned into June, they were good for a seven-game advantage over number-two Montreal. Going into July, the Phillies' .675 winning percentage still topped every club in baseball, but their Achilles heel was shortstop, and everyone knew it.

Juan Bell filled the slot at the start of the season. Because of inconsistent and sometimes maddeningly lackluster play, as well as a .200 batting average, Juan found he was indeed the one for whom the bell tolled. He was put on waivers and on June 1st the Milwaukee Brewers nabbed him. That left the shortstop position open for Mariano Duncan and Kim Batiste. Neither made the local fans forget the bygone Days of Wine and Rojas as well as Ruben Amaro (Gold Glove winner at short in 1964), when superb glove work at shortstop was a given in Philadelphia. Did I mention a shortstop named Bowa?

As *Philadelphia Daily News* writer Paul Hagan recaps the situation, "Lee Thomas decided to bring up Kevin Stocker when he watched two ground balls roll past Kim Batiste for hits in the fifth inning of a loss to the Dodgers. When the game ended, Thomas bolted into Fregosi's office and said, 'You're getting a new shortstop.

Look, I'm the guy who made the decision, so give me all the grief if it doesn't work out.'"

The call to the minors was made. Stocker reported to the park for the first time on July 7, 1993 in the midst of a heavy-duty pennant race that had all of Philadelphia going wild for its Phillies.

THE GAME OF MY LIFE
JULY 7, 1993
BY KEVIN STOCKER

It was a thrill coming up to the Phillies at that point in time. I knew the expectations for me were high and so was the responsibility. That '93 Phillies clubhouse was completely unique. Those guys were all about winning baseball games. They had their fun, but winning was what they were about. I felt good about that attitude because the only way I've ever played is all out, so I wasn't intimidated. Besides, guys like Larry Andersen welcomed me as soon as I arrived and made me feel part of the club.

I was put right into the starting lineup. That was a thrill and my first game turned out to be one of the most memorable of that crazy year. Nobody scored in the first inning, although we did threaten. It seems we were always threatening that year. That team kept coming at an opponent. In the bottom of the second, the game was scoreless when we came to bat. I was batting behind Mickey Morandini, who walked to start the inning.

In my first plate appearance, I followed Mickey's walk with a walk. That put me on first and Mickey on second with no outs. Then we made a couple of outs before Milt Thompson came through. Milt hit kind of a weak pop fly to left. It landed in the right spot for a double. Mickey and I both scored to put us up 2–0. I came to the plate again the following inning. This time I wasn't so lucky. I struck out against Ramon Martinez. The game stayed close until, a couple of innings later, Krukker hit one out of the park and we were up 4–1.

The Dodgers kept coming back though. They came within a run of us before we got another homer (the Dude, Lenny Dykstra) and stretched the lead out again to a couple of runs 5–3—that's the way it stayed until the ninth. Then Mitch Williams came in and walked the Dodgers' leadoff man. A single and a couple of walks later and the score was 5–4. Mitch was yanked out of the game and Larry Andersen relieved him. Eric Karros singled in the tying run, and his hit put the Dodgers on second and third.

That's when Mike Piazza hit a ball to short. I fielded it and threw to the plate for a force out to preserve the tie. Larry got the next two guys out. We went down in the second half of the ninth and loaded the bases.

I came up a few innings later in the 12th with a chance to win the game. Morandini was on third, he had stolen second base and advanced to third on Piazza's inerrant throw, but I grounded out to second and the game wore on.

We were really chewing up our bullpen in the game. Eventually, in the 15th inning Mike Williams came on and did a super job from then on out. The game stayed tied all the way up to the 20th and Mike pitched the whole way for us. In the bottom of the 20th, I had a chance to do something good. Eisenreich had led off with a single. Morandini followed with another single to center so Eisey had to stop at second. I was called on to lay down a sacrifice. Eisey got a great jump and made it to third, so the sacrifice was successful. Then I think Kim Batiste popped up and Lenny Dykstra followed with a huge double to win the game—the long, long game. What a debut. I'll never forget it.

One of the more interesting sidelights of the night was that I didn't have any of my own bats. I borrowed Dave Hollins' bat because it was the closest to the style I used. I didn't know how touchy he was and how superstitious all those guys were. Dave was genuinely concerned that I was stealing his hits.

WRAPPING IT UP

"After the game, Jim Fregosi called me into his office," Stocker chuckles. "The coaching staff was worried about my batting stroke. They thought I had changed it. Fregosi asked me, 'What are you doing at the plate? You weren't swinging like that when we saw you in spring training!' I was a little surprised since I thought I was called up to the Phillies mostly for defense and to help stabilize the middle infield. So much for my hitting not being important! Anyway, we straightened things out and I had decent success at the plate that season."

As for the game, the marathon lasted six hours and 20 minutes.

"The night before Stocker arrived," adds Larry Andersen, "we were all in the trainer's room saying we had to give the kid a lot of encouragement. To the greatest extent anyone in that clubhouse could do it, we wanted to make it easy on the kid. Then we saw how tough Kevin was and he was accepted right away as one of us. The downside for Stocker is that his acceptance made him eligible for some other 'stuff.' I'll tell you one thing we did to Kevin. A few weeks after that long Dodger game, we had a flight to San Diego. I told Stock he had to put on a smock and serve everyone like a flight attendant. His name was 'Colleen' for the flight and, typical for Kevin Stocker, he did a great job. Actually, Irish Mike Ryan, who because he was imbibing during the flight, his vision might not have been quite up to snuff, nudged Fregosi at one point and said, 'That stewardess looks a lot like Stocker.'"

"Stocker did great," continues Andersen on the Dodger 20-inning game. "It was Mitch I was worried about. Kruk and Daulton and the rest of the guys were looking forward to getting into the clubhouse for a few brews after the ninth inning. Of course, that didn't happen. The Dodgers scored those runs off Mitch. The next day when I came into the clubhouse, I figured Kruk, Daulton and those guys might have killed Mitch. The first thing I did was to go to my locker and see if there was a black arm patch sewn on my sleeve with 'Number 99' (Mitch's jersey number) on it."

CHAPTER 17

RYNE DUREN

"I pitched in some big games," says Ryne Duren. "In the '58 World Series, I took a loss in Game 1 when Billy Bruton singled in a run on me. But in Game 6 I came into the game in the fifth, pitched until the tenth and got the win. A few games in Philadelphia come to mind as the game of my life—one against the Giants, the other against the Mets. I had some good games as a Phillie. I had my greatest success in New York with the Yankees, but I had some success here for Gene Mauch and the Phils too."

MEET RYNE DUREN

Rinold George Duren was signed as a 20-year-old free agent by the old St. Louis Browns. Ryne had been such a hard thrower in high school that his coaches made him play second base.

"I pitched batting practice one time and broke a kid's ribs," Duren recalls. "They didn't let me pitch after that. They wouldn't let me play short or third either, because I threw the ball so hard across the infield, I might have hurt somebody in the stands if it went wild. It might even hurt the first baseman. I couldn't play outfield 'cause my eyesight was too bad to pick up the ball. So they put me at second base where I could flip the ball underhand to first base."

Duren made his debut on the last day of the '54 season when the Baltimore Orioles, who had been the St. Louis Browns prior to coming to Baltimore, dropped an 11–0 laugher to Billy Pierce and the Chicago White Sox. It was the Orioles' 100th loss for the season.

"My real debut was on May 10, 1957," Duren points out. "I had been traded to the Kansas City Athletics in late September '56 and I was starting against the Yankees. The first guy I faced was Hank Bauer. He had to hit the dirt on my first three pitches. They weren't malicious—I just didn't have good control. I hit the outside corner the next three pitches and struck him out. Gil McDougald came up next and I struck him out. Back in the dugout, their manager Casey Stengel was asking them, 'What's going on?' They said, 'Casey, we're married guys with family and kids. This guy's throwing 100 MPH. You'd better either get him for us or get him out of the league!' So the Yankees got me."

They traded Billy Martin, Ralph Terry, Woodie Held, and Bob Martin for Ryne, Jim Pisoni and Harry Simpson. The Yankees sent Duren to AAA-Denver for seasoning. In his first start he threw a no-hitter.

"They said it was the only no-hitter by a home-team pitcher in the history of pro baseball in Denver," he says.

Duren went 13–2 and saved more than ten games. His two losses came in 1–0 games, and both times the runs were unearned. Still the Yankees didn't bring him up until the following season.

"It was tough to crack the big leagues in those days," he chuckles.

Duren considers the 1959 campaign his best ever. It was one of only two seasons in the fifties that the "Damn Yankees" did not win the pennant.

"The day we were eliminated from the pennant my ERA was 0.68," he reveals. "In one stretch that year, I pitched 37 innings without giving up a run. But believe it or not, the New York Yankees went 45 innings without getting me a run."

Stengel, always good for a laugh, once told reporters, "We had this guy who couldn't see good, and what they did was send him to these fancy New York doctors. He got seeing so good that he was grooving the ball right down the middle all the time. They started hitting him." When the writers asked if he was talking about Duren, the Ol' Perfessor said he was. "But," the writers countered, "He's pitching really well. How did that happen?" Casey replied, "I just took a dirty handkerchief out to him."

In 1963, Gene Mauch brought Duren to Philly.

Ryne Duren terrified hitters because of his poor vision, poor control, and 100-mph fastball. *Photograph by Brace Photos*

"He ran into me in Florida during spring training," recalls Duren. "I was playing more golf than pitching, but he got the Phillies to purchase my contract. I always got along well with Mauch. I know he wanted a veteran to solidify that team—somebody who would be a good influence on the bench. I came over to the Phillies later in spring training. I don't think I gave up a run. I was throwing well."

Duren threw well enough to tally a 6–2 record with a 3.30 ERA and 84 whiffs in 87 ⅓ innings of work.

"I enjoyed my time in Philly," says Duren. "I liked playing for Mauch. He was one of those managers that kept a team in the game—meaning he kept everybody's head in the game. He'd go down the bench and keep everybody alert, asking guys what they would do in certain situations. I didn't last long in '64. I was gone by May. The Phils traded me to Cincinnati. You know, I talked to Mauch the next year and he told me he thought I could have been the difference for the Phils, if I had stayed the year with them. I was a spot starter and I was still throwing well. When he kind of got low on pitching down that last stretch, he thought I could have been an answer. I don't know why I was let go either. I was throwing well. In fact, I had developed a pretty good sinker and slider. I was throwing the breaking stuff and Mauch gave it to me good one day, 'I want you throwing smoke out there, not breaking balls!' So I did and I had a good year in '63."

Duren had a good stint with the Reds in '64. He was 0–2 as a Red but flashed a nifty 2.88 ERA. In '65, he came back to Philly but was released and signed by the Washington Senators. The Senators released him by the end of August and that was it. Duren was out of baseball. Wildness had kept him from achieving his full potential. He was the definitive power pitcher. In 589 career innings, he fanned 630 batters. He also issued 392 walks, plunked 48 wobbly-kneed batters and uncorked 38 wild pitches.

After retirement, he continued battling the other enemy that impeded his march to superstardom—alcoholism. From the late '60s through 1972, he was a counselor-supervisor at the Norris Foundation in Mukwonago, Wisconsin. In 1972, Duren developed and directed the Stoughton Community Hospital Alcohol Rehabilitation and Education Program in Stoughton, Wisconsin. He remained director of that program until 1980, and then served as a consultant on alcohol and drug abuse to numerous community agencies, associations, and professional sports organizations. He also served on the Wisconsin Governor's Citizen Advisory Committee on

Alcohol Abuse and the new Wisconsin Drinking and Driving Council.

Duren has published two books, *Comeback* and *I Can See Clearly Now* that chronicle his battles and suggest methods of controlling the disease. He also heads up the Winning Beyond Winning Foundation that provides cross-training for kids in metropolitan New York. The group emphasizes social skills, manners, alcohol, and drug education and awareness.

As Duren emphasizes, "I'm not anti-alcohol. I'm pro-education. I think drinking and alcohol belong, but you can't use them ignorantly."

SETTING THE STAGE

As the saying goes, "Good pitching always beats good hitting. And vice versa." In the year 1963, the first proposition ruled. The Dodgers won the National League pennant by six games. The San Francisco Giants finished a distant third, 11 games off the mark with the Phillies right on their tail, 12 games behind L.A. Young fans can't appreciate how astonishing the Giants' third-place finish was. How does a team with three Hall of Famers in their three-four-five slots (Willie McCovey, Willie Mays, and Orlando Cepeda) finish any place but first? Pitching you say? The Giants' pitching staff consisted of 1957 Rookie of the Year (as a Phil) Jack Sanford, Hall of Famer Juan Marichal, and 14–10 Billy O'Dell—not too shabby. Yet San Francisco hurlers couldn't match the Dodgers' star-studded staff headed by Hall of Famers, Don Drysdale and Sandy Koufax.

In any event, the '63 Phils were holding their own against the Giants, who had come to town in mid-July for a big four-game series. The Giants were always a big draw in the Quaker City (any time Willie Mays came to any town so did the fans). After three games, the young Fightins had beaten San Francisco two games to one. The loss was no shame. They lost to Marichal, who went 25–8 that year. Philadelphia had gone 5–2 the previous week and needed a win as a confidence-builder.

"Before each series, the coaches, catchers, and pitchers got together and talked about how to pitch each guy," Ryne Duren explains. "I remember talking about the Giants. They had all those great hitters. I said I usually had luck against Willie Mays. I was more leery of McCovey. He was hot at the time and we spent a lot of time trying to figure out how to get him out. I said, 'The way he digs in with that big left foot—he takes over the plate. I'm gonna throw him something that makes him lift that big foot up and loosen him up there.' I was a spot starter for Mauch. He wanted this game and he gave me the start. I had mostly been working out of the bullpen. So I went out and tried to pick up the win."

THE GAME OF MY LIFE
JULY 13, 1963
BY RYNE DUREN

We were playing on a hot summer day in Philly. The stands weren't too full (attendance was only 10,452—a typical Saturday afternoon crowd in the era). Well, I got the first two guys out with no trouble, then McCovey steps up. I wanted to brush him back a bit, but I plunked him right on the shin. He didn't like it. He ran down to first. It had to hurt him. Of course, he wouldn't rub it, but then he took a step off the bag and plop—he fainted. I thought they had to take him out of the game, but he hung in. The next inning or so, they moved Willie to left field. I think he switched positions with Cepeda.

We won the game. Roy Sievers sort of took care of that himself. You know, I just saw Sievers up at a golf outing. He was signing autographs. He's doing well. I've got to tell you a little story though. He sort of 'carried the piano' when he ran, if you know what I mean. I was sitting in the bullpen one game when Roy was on first base. Somebody hit a ball down to the bullpen. I just sat there, making it tough for the outfielder to find the ball, buying time for Roy to score from first. Well the outfielder finally found it. I looked up, expecting that Roy would be crossing the plate. But he absolutely ran out of gas rounding third. About 20 feet down the baseline, he stumbled and started crawling toward the plate. He was out by 15 feet. Normally that would have frosted Mauch and he would have been right over to Sievers when he hit the bench. But Mauch was laughing his head off in the dugout. It looked so comical.

Anyway that day, Sievers hit a couple of home runs. We scored four. I held them to three—two of them came on a Willie Mays homer—and that's how the game ended, 4–3.

Later that season, I was pitching against the Giants in relief. We had a slim lead and up steps Mays. Mauch comes to the mound. I didn't want to get yanked, so we talked. Mauch says, "Throw the

SOB three spitters." I threw the occasional spitter. Imagine me, when I was an alcoholic, wetting one up! Well I threw him two spitters. The third hardly moved and Willie hit it like a one-iron shot and almost carried our shortstop Bobby Wine to the outfield. But we beat the Giants again.

WRAPPING IT UP

Three days later, the Phillies launched into a seven-game winning streak. A month later they had battled from eighth place to fourth, but that would be as high as they got.

Meanwhile in Kansas City on July 13, 1962, in the second game of a doubleheader, Cleveland's Early Wynn left the game with a lead after having struggled through five innings. Four scoreless relief innings by Jerry Walker gave Wynn his 300th career victory 7–4. It had taken Wynn eight unsuccessful tries for the elusive 300th and final career win.

CHAPTER 18

LARRY ANDERSEN

"I've been thinking about it since you asked me," says Larry Andersen when asked to choose the game of his life. "And I keep coming up with the same one. It has to be game five of that 1993 NLCS. I got my only save of the year, threw a pitch that I never threw in a game either before or after, and somehow struck two guys out."

MEET LARRY ANDERSEN

Larry Andersen, or "LA" as his friends call him, has been a Philly homeboy for more than two decades. His reputation for wild and wacky pranks and practical jokes is hard earned and well deserved. Larry once pulled off the prank forever known in baseball circles as 'Jellogate.' Andersen, Richie Zisk, and Joe Simpson conned the team's traveling secretary into giving them the key to manager Rene Lachmann's hotel room.

"We consumed some adult beverages," says Andersen. "We went into Lach's room, and made it look like a sort of localized hurricane had hit it. We put all the mattresses and bedding material in one of the two bathrooms. We removed all the lights from the fixtures, changed the times on the clocks and took the mouthpiece out of the phone. Then we put eight boxes of jello in each toilet and encouraged the jelloing process by pouring generous quantities of ice into the water.

"Next day at the park, Lach was still fuming and cussing and threatening to call the FBI to have the place dusted for fingerprints.

For the rest of the year, we had room service deliver him jello every night. We even broke into the little refrigerator in the manager's room in the clubhouse. We poked holes in the bottom of the beer cans, emptied the beer, and replaced it with jello. Ten years later, we had hats made up. We wrapped a label, "Mr. Jello's 10-year Anniversary" around a box of jello."

In the wacky clubhouse of 1993's "Beards, Bellies, and Biceps" squad, Larry found his element and quickly hit his stride. As a veteran, he played a key role in developing and honing the team's unique chemistry. He also kept an intense team loose and helped make the baseball experience, almost to a man, impossible to replicate.

Andersen looks back on his '93 days as the zenith of a career that started on September 5, 1975, when he relieved for Cleveland in a game against Detroit.

"The Tigers had blown the game wide open with a big inning in the fifth," he recalls. "Frank Robinson our manager was beside himself so he put me in."

LA had the right stuff, setting the Tigers down 1-2-3, and ringing up Aurelio Rodriguez for his first major-league whiff. Apparently in Cleveland, nothing impedes like success. That was the last Major League action Larry saw until 1977 when Cleveland brought him up to the bigs for good. Andersen had been a 22-year-old kid in his debut. When he walked off the field for the last time on July 31, 1994 as a Phillie, he was 41 years old—the second oldest guy in the NL.

In between those two events, he enjoyed a pretty fine career and posted some impressive numbers. He pitched 101⅔ innings of relief in 1987 for Houston. He logged back-to-back campaigns where his ERA was less than 2.00 (1.54 ERA in 1989, 1.79 ERA in 1990). He boasted a 2.25 ERA for the Phillies in postseason play in 1983. In 1984, he set the Phillies club record for most consecutive scoreless innings by a reliever (33 IP). That number still rates second-place on the Phillies all-time list for scoreless innings. The first name on the list is the immortal Grover Cleveland Alexander. Larry also played in two World Series as a Phillie (1983 and 1993), and four League Championship Series—two with the Phillies, one for the Astros (1986), and one for the BoSox (1990).

Noted for his devil-may-care, friendly style, Andersen made a smooth transition to his post-active playing career. He spent three

Larry Andersen, prankster extraordinaire, was the chief perpetrator of baseball's shameful jello-gate scandal. *Gary Newkirk/Getty Images*

years as a minor-league pitching coach with AA Reading (1995-'96) and Scranton (1997). In 1997, he was offered a Houston Astros broadcasting job when Larry Dierker moved from the booth back to the field. Dierker turned it down and opted for the job of Phillies pitching coach.

The next year, however, he decided to change career direction and launched his career in the booth. He has been there ever since.

Andersen is also well known to the waves of happy campers who head south for the Phillies Fantasy Camp in Clearwater each winter. He's especially famous (or infamous) to the night owls and beer-lovers, who have played hard in Clearwater and lived to tell about it. That's the crew of campers that return to the Delaware Valley in desperate need of a vacation and sleep.

SETTING THE STAGE

It was the NLCS with the Braves. We had taken Atlanta in the opener at the Vet in extra innings. They crushed us in the second game though, and we were off to Atlanta for game three. They beat us pretty good again (9–4). Then Danny Jackson pitched the game of his life.   And the series was even—two games apiece. We were headed into our final game in Atlanta. Curt Schilling, who was really emerging as a big-game pitcher, was going for us. We were a confident bunch anyway—that '93 team.

The Story of the 1993 Philadelphia Phillies titled, *More Than Beards, Bellies, and Biceps—and the Phillies Phanatic Too*, gives a detailed account of this wacky team—and does justice to Jackson's performance.

THE GAME OF MY LIFE
OCTOBER 11, 1993
BY LARRY ANDERSEN

Steve Avery was on the hill for Atlanta. We jumped out to a lead in the first. I think Krukker knocked the run in. Then we added a couple more. I know Dutch (catcher Darren Daulton) got one of them with a homer. We went into the bottom of the ninth with a 3–0 lead. The inning didn't start off well. Schilling walked Otis Nixon to lead off. Then poor Batty (Kim Batiste who had been inserted at third base as a defensive replacement for Dave Hollins) blew a double-play

130

ball. Schilling had two on and no outs with the tying run at the plate and 60,000 people doing that chop thing they do down there.

Fregosi brought in Mitch Williams to face Ron Gant, who greeted him with a single to make the game 3–1—still no out. David Justice hit a sac fly to make it 3–2 with one out. Then Terry Pendleton singled and runners were on the corners. Francisco Cabrera, the same guy who won the NLCS for the Braves a year before, singled to tie the game. That was it, though. Mitch struck out Mark Lemke, and Bill Pecota flied out.

"We came up in the top of the tenth. Atlanta had that fire-baller, Mark Wohlers, on the mound. Lenny Dykstra, the Dude, hit a 2–2 pitch about 400 feet, and we had the lead, 4–3.

Mitch was the closer and he was out of the game, so Fregosi put me in. I was barking at that point. I didn't have anything left. My slider was moving but it wasn't breaking down, so I was in jeopardy every time I got the ball up. I was facing the top of their order. Otis Nixon flied out, but he hit it to the warning track. I was a little worried. Then I got Blauser on a slider that was belt high. I think Dutch was worried at that point too.

Ron Gant, a guy with tremendous power came up, and I slipped a couple strikes past him. Then, when I was ahead in the count, Dutch called for a split-finger fastball. I couldn't believe my eyes. I was so used to seeing him throw a couple of fingers down for the slider. I had no idea what he was doing. I had experimented with a split-finger fastball on the sidelines but I never threw one in a game. I didn't know if Dutch called it because my slider was so bad, or because he figured we could surprise Gant. I never asked him, but I think I know what he'd say. The pitch started up and away and came back and caught the corner and Gant was caught looking.

I didn't know what to do when I walked off the mound. I was as surprised as anyone. But I had my first save of the season—pretty good time to get it. And we were headed back to Philly ahead 3–2 in the NLCS.

WRAPPING IT UP

Today, Fregosi still shakes his head, "Andy was just about barking that fifth game. I knew that, but I had to put him in. That last pitch to Gant—I'll never forget it. He kept shaking off signs and I thought, 'Something's going on here.' Then he throws Gant a split-fingered fastball. Here's the thing—that is a pitch Larry Andersen did not have. He was making things up as he went along. I think Gant was in a state of shock because he was looking for a slider away and he just watched that split-finger pass him by for a strike."

"I asked LA after the game," added John Kruk. "'What the hell kind of a pitch was that?' He told me it was a forkball. I said, 'I didn't think you had one of those,' and he answered, 'Neither did I!' Can you imagine that? The guy's out there experimenting with pitches in the NLCS!"

The Phillies went on to win the NLCS two nights later in Philadelphia. And did Larry Andersen, who had never thrown a split-fingered fastball in a game situation before, go on to become even more feared and dangerous by adding a new pitch to his repertoire?

"No," Andersen says. "I never threw another one again."

CHAPTER 19

JERRY MARTIN

"I wasn't a big star for the Phillies," says Jerry Martin. "But I played on some good teams and I put in some good days wearing that uniform. I had a few two-homer games in my career. I guess the game of my life would be the day I hit a grand slam that beat the Dodgers at Dodger Stadium."

MEET JERRY MARTIN

"I was a Yankee fan growing up," Martin confesses. How did a kid born and raised in Columbia South Carolina end up loving the hated Yankees?

"It was the sixties," Martin explains. "We didn't see much major-league baseball in South Carolina in those days. It seemed like every time a game was broadcast, the Yankees were on the tube. Tresh, Mantle, Maris and those Yankee guys are the guys I watched all the time, so the Yankees became my team."

After starring in high school, Martin went on to become the biggest major-league star that Furman University in Greenville, South Carolina ever produced. The Phillies drafted him in '71 and after putting in a few years in the minors, he debuted with the Phillies in September 1974.

"I had a big thrill practically right off the bat," says Martin. "In my first big-league at-bat, I got what turned out to be the game-winning hit at St. Louis off John Curtis. When I reached first base after the hit, Joe Torre, who was playing first, said, 'Nice hit.' Jim Lonborg shut the Cards out that night. So all in one night, I got my first big-league start in centerfield, my first hit and my first game-winning hit. That was all pretty memorable."

Martin served as a defensive replacement for Greg Luzinski from '75 until '79 when he departed Philadelphia. The Furman product also spelled some of the left-handed bats in the outfield like Del Unser and Bake McBride when the Phillies faced portsiders.

"In the '78 NLCS against the Dodgers, I had a thrill in the first game," says Martin. "Unfortunately, it was only a personal thrill. I hit a homer off the Dodgers' Bob Welch. I pinch hit for Tug McGraw in the ninth with one out and no one on. We were down 9–4 at the time. We didn't score any more after my homer and the game ended 9–5. You know how the series ended, so I won't go into that—that's not a happy memory.

"I remember another big game in Houston in '78," he adds. "I came in to pinch hit in the top of the ninth for Richie Hebner because Joe Sambito, a lefty, was pitching. Ken Forsch had started for Houston, but we knocked him out. The game was tied at five. In the ninth, after Larry Bowa led off with a single, Schmidt fanned. Then José Cardenal singled. I came up and hit one out for a three-run homer. We were only a game up in the standings so it gave me a good feeling of contributing."

After the '78 season, Martin was traded to the Cubs along with Henry Mack, Derek Botello, Barry Foote, and Ted Sizemore. In return, the Phillies got Manny Trillo, Dave Rader, and Greg Gross. Following the trade, Jerry became a starter for the first and only time in his career. He responded by slamming 19 homers in his first year in the Windy City followed by 23 in 1980.

After the '80 season, Martin was dealt to the Giants where he spent a year as a spot starter. At season's end, he was goin' to Kansas City, where he slammed 15 homers in his last season as a starter. At season's end, he was granted free agency and was signed by the Mets. He spent his final year in the bigs in New York where he registered only 91 at-bats and batted .206.

He began his coaching career in 1990 with the Phillies as a coach for Martinsville; Jerry assures us the town was not named in his honor. From 1991 to 1998 he was the roving hitting instructor in the

Jerry Martin was an able replacement—both offensively and defensively—for the Phillies in the 1970s. *Photograph by Brace Photos*

Phillies minor league system. He returned to coaching at Piedmont in 1999–2000. After that stint, he served in AAA-Scranton from 2001 to 2003. Since 2004, he has been the outfield, base-running coordinator for the Phillies minor league system.

SETTING THE STAGE

With their 80–82 slate in 1974, Phillies showed a lot of promise. Consider the seasons that immediately preceded it: 1969 (63–99), 1970 (73–88), 1971 (67–95), 1972 (59–97), and 1973 (71–91).

To a loss-glutted city, the '74 Phillies looked like the second coming of Murderer's Row. Thus the '74 edition of the Phillies lifted Quaker City hopes more than any other Phillies team since, dare we say, the '64 squad.

In 1975, the Phillies fulfilled their obligatory opening-day loss. Tom Seaver and the Mets bested Steve Carlton and the Phillies 2–1. The opener out of the way, the Phils then flirted with .500 mark for a month before hitting it for the first time on May 3. They managed to stay on the good side of that benchmark for the rest of the season.

By June 12, they were rolling along with a 31–27 record, only 1½ games behind Pittsburgh's Lightning and Lumber Gang. Walter Alston's Dodgers were coasting along at a 34–28 pace, which earned them second place in the Western Division, 3½ games behind Cincinnati's Big Red Machine. That was the league landscape as the Phillies prepped for Friday the thirteenth.

THE GAME OF MY LIFE
JUNE 13, 1975
BY JERRY MARTIN

We were in third place at game time. We could just feel this team coming of age. In '74, we had a losing record, but guys like Greg Luzinski, Mike Schmidt, and Dave Cash, were blossoming into stars. Lefty was our stopper but we also had Jim Lonborg, who was a good pitcher. Dick Allen was on the team too. He gave us a veteran presence that helped our young team. We were starting to believe in ourselves.

We were playing in Dodger Stadium—always a tough place for a visiting team to win a ballgame. I started in centerfield. Garry Maddox had recently come to the Phillies from the Giants (on May 4, 1975) and claimed that starting job. So this night was a rarity for me, getting a chance to start.

The Dodgers scored in the bottom of the first. I think Davey Lopes got on base and stole second. Then he scored on a double. The game settled into a pitchers' duel. In our half of the seventh, we got things going. Our catcher, Johnny Oates led off with a single. Mike Schmidt sacrifice-bunted him to second. Schmidty wasn't called on to sacrifice bunt too many times more in his career, was he?

Then Luzinski and Allen singled and we scored. Tony Taylor walked and loaded the bases for me. I stepped in to face Andy Messerschmidt, who had been pitching great not only that night but for the entire season up to that point (Messerschmidt was 9–2 going into the game). He served one up that I saw real good and I connected well enough to drive it out. That was my first and only big-league grand slam. It put us up 5–1. Yeah, it was quite a thrill for a young guy like me to do that while I was playing with all the great players on that '75 roster.

That wrapped up the scoring for the game. Lonborg pitched the final two innings and we wound up winning 5–1. I knew at the time that I had just played a game I was going to remember a long time.

WRAPPING IT UP

A week later the Phillies had advanced from third place to second. They remained in second for the duration of the season with the exception of four scattered days in September. Philadelphia recorded an 86–76 record for the season. Most important, they maintained that momentum right on through the following season, when they ended up winning more games in a season than any other Philadelphia Phillies team before or since.

CHAPTER 20

RUBEN AMARO SR.

"Even though we lost this particular game," says Ruben Amaro Sr. about the game of his life, "I'd have to pick the game we lost to St. Louis prior to our 10-game losing streak in 1964. Everyone knows that losing streak hurt, but the game we lost to the Cardinals a few weeks before that, kind of set us up for that collapse."

MEET RUBEN AMARO SR.

"I grew up where Bobby Avila grew up," says Ruben Amaro Sr.

Bobby Avila was a member of the 1954 Cleveland Indian American League pennant winners. Avila won the league batting title that year. Amaro was a promising hitter as a young Mexican prospect in the early fifties.

"I don't know what happened," Amaro chuckles. "When I was young and first got into organized ball, I was a good hitter."

That's when the athletic 5-foot-11, 170 pound, 18-year-old Cardinal prospect, Ruben Amaro, met the colorful Cardinal player-manager Harry "The Hat" Walker. "Harry Walker started working with me when I started with the Cardinal organization," says Amaro. "He stressed fielding so much I forgot about hitting."

Harry the Hat managed the St. Louis Cardinals for one year (1955) in the fifties. The Cardinals had signed Amaro before the 1955 season as an amateur free agent. He paid his dues in the minors for a few years—finally making his major league debut on June 29, 1958.

"I got into the second game of a doubleheader against the Phils at Connie Mack Stadium," he recalls.

Amaro was a defensive replacement for Johnny O'Brien in that game. He appeared in 39 other games on a Cardinal team that featured the likes of Hall of Famer Stan Musial, Ken Boyer, ex-Philadelphia legend Del Ennis, Curt Flood, Wilmer David "Vinegar Bend" Mizell, Blazer Blasingame, Lindy McDaniel, Sad Sam Jones, and Wally Moon (a year before he started launching his Moon Shots in L.A.). With that cast, the Cards couldn't even manage a first-division finish.

The following year, Amaro was in the Phillies organization. The popular Chico Fernandez was the Phillies' regular shortstop in 1958. His popularity accrued mostly in 1957 when Chico was one of the Phillies' promising Fabulous Four Freshman—Jack Sanford, Harry "The Horse" Anderson, Ed Bouchee, and Fernandez. Each of the quartet, save for Jack Sanford and Ed Bouchee, turned out to be a mere flash. Sanford's flash was exhibited on the diamond, Bouchee's off.

Fernandez was shipped to Detroit in '59 and his vacated shortstop slot was filled by Joe Koppe (who teamed with Sparky Anderson at second base in Sparky's less than spectacular one-year career as a Phillie), while Ruben spent another year in the minors. In '59, Ruben was called up to the majors for good. He wrested the starting shortstop away from Koppe and retained it for the next two seasons in 1961 and 1962. Then an interesting quirk occurred. History records Bobby Wine as the official "regular" shortstop for the remainder of Ruben's tenure in Philly, which extended through the '65 campaign. Wine's "regular" status didn't prevent Amaro from winning the National League Gold Glove Award at shortstop in '64—one year after Bobby Wine had won the same award as shortstop. In fact, when Wine won his Gold Glove in 1963, he became the first Phillie ever to win a Gold Glove.

"Yes," Amaro smiles. "I won the award after Bobby. We were always good friends and he's one of the guys I'm good friends with yet. We still keep in touch. But I think the way that happened—the way I got the Award in '64—was that I started a lot of games at shortstop, but then later in the game, (manager) Gene Mauch would

---

Ruben Amaro Sr. was a slick fielder who won a gold glove at shortstop in the Phillies' infamous 1964 campaign. *Photograph by Brace Photos*

shift me to a different position, like first base or third base. Or I would start a different position and then move to shortstop late in the game. Anyway, I was honored to receive the Gold Glove Award." In that ill-fated year of 1964, Amaro not only won the Gold Glove Award at shortstop, he finished 21st in the MVP voting. That's an unusual feat for a guy who batted .264. However, the honor is made even more meaningful given that he only played in 129 games that season.

After the 1965 campaign, Amaro was traded to the Yankees. He arrived after the Yankee Dynasty had crumbled. Only two years before, they lost a hard-fought World Series to the St. Louis Cardinals in the suddenly dominant National League. In '66, Mickey Mantle socked only 23 homers; Roger Maris, 13. Switch-hitting Horace Clarke was the starting shortstop on the '66 Yankees. However, in a year of multiple personnel changes, Clarke, a Virgin Island native, was shifted to second base in '67. Clarke replaced another Yankee legend, Bobby Richardson, who retired at the age of 30. Clarke's shift left the shortstop position open for Amaro, who played 130 games that year.

The "Bronx Bomber" tag that the Yankees held for so long took on a different meaning. "Bomb" came to mean bomb as in what the Edsel did. If that's an arcane reference for more modern readers, consider "bomb" as in the Benifer merger or the Brittney-Kfed union. In current lingo, the Yanks were no longer "The Bomb" in the American League. The once-mighty Bombers plummeted to a ninth-place, one-step-from-the-basement finish. Nonetheless, one year later Amaro lost his starting shortstop position to 24-year-old Tom Tresh—a guy who would become another Yankee legend.

In November '68, Ruben was purchased from the Yanks by the California Angels. Amaro batted only 27 times with the Angels in 1969, which proved to be his final year as an active major-league player. The Phils signed him as a free agent on April 13, 1970; however, Ruben never made it up to the Phils again as a player. Subsequently he did work for the Phils in a number of other capacities. The most visible and certainly the most memorable was his role as coach on the 1980 World Champions.

Ruben's son, Ruben Amaro Jr., is currently the Phillies' assistant general manager. Ruben Sr. is the supervisor for Latin American Affairs for the Chicago White Sox.

SETTING THE STAGE

"We were in Los Angeles for a three-game series," remembers Ruben Amaro Sr. "We were in the midst of that western swing as they call it. We played in Houston and we took the series there. We owned Houston that year."

The '64 Phillies did what winning teams do—they cleaned up on the bottom-dwellers and topped Houston 13–5 in the season series while stomping the last-place Mets 15–3.

"Our success against Houston (and New York) had a lot to do with our overall success," continues Amaro Sr. "As I always say, we played great ball for 146 games that year. Unfortunately, the season was (and still is) 162 games long. This game was one of the 146-games group when we were playing well. Still, it seems something went out of us after we lost this game.

"On that western swing, we took the series in Houston," says Amaro. "Then we went to San Francisco and took that series. Next, it was Los Angeles where we dropped two of three. I think we were a little tired at that point and it didn't help that we had to hop on a plane and fly across the country to Philadelphia for a Wednesday night game at Connie Mack Stadium. We were tired but happy to be home. We had a good crowd coming to cheer us, and things had been going our way up until then.

The attendance was 25,339—a great Wednesday night crowd in those days. The Phillies entered the game with an 83–56 record and a comfortable six-game lead.

THE GAME OF MY LIFE
SEPTEMBER 9, 1964
BY RUBEN AMARO SR.

We started the game well. Curt Simmons was pitching for the Cards. Bunning was our starter. We both scored in the first. In the second inning, we put together a few hits and a walk and went ahead 2–1. Johnny Callison hit a big double for us a few innings later and we lengthened the lead (Phils 4 – Cards 1, after four innings). Then they got a couple back. We added an insurance run in the eighth. That inning, I had gotten my third hit of the night (all singles). Then Jack Baldschun, who had relieved Bunning three innings earlier, doubled and put us on top 5–3. I scored that insurance run.

Jack (Baldschun) was a good pitcher. We thought we were in good shape with him on the mound and a two-run lead in the ninth. We weren't. A kind of freak play nearly ruined the game.

A guy named Charlie James got a single pinch-hitting for their pitcher (Barney Schultz). Then Curt Flood grounded out. We forced James at second, but Curt could run well and we didn't turn two. That turned out to be big. Lou Brock followed with a single that moved Curt to third, but this was the key play. On that single, Brock overran first. We had him hung up between first and second. Danny Cater was playing first at the time. Danny wasn't our starting first baseman. Unfortunately, he wasn't as familiar with playing first base as some of the other guys on the team. He was too concerned with Flood over there on third base and he let Brock scoot back to first safely. If we had gotten Brock out, we would have had two outs and only one guy on with a two-run lead. Instead, with that one critical turn of events, we wound up with two guys on and only one out.

A pitch or two later, Brock was on second with a steal. Lou was en route to 58 steals for the season (the biggest steal in the '64 season, however, was the trade the Cards engineered with the Cubs to bring Brock to St. Louis on June 15, 1964).

Bill White grounded out and Flood scored to cut our lead to one. Brock went to third on the play. Now, we only needed one more out to win the game. Ken Boyer was up. He was a really great player and was having a great year (Boyer won the MVP in '64 with Johnny Callison as the runner-up). This time, Boyer got lucky. He threw the bat at the ball and managed to hit it. Baldschun had some really great breaking pitches and Boyer was fooled. The bat and the ball both went out toward the pitcher and somehow, Boyer safely made it to first. Brock scored to tie the game. The next guy (shortstop Dick Groat) made an out and we went into extra innings.

Neither team scored the next inning, but the Cards came up with a big inning in the 11th and it was the same guys who hurt us. Flood led off with a single. Brock followed with a single. Then Bill White doubled them both home. Ed Roebuck replaced Baldschun. They bunched some more hits. Dick Allen made an error at third and when it was all over, we were down 10–5. Unfortunately, after getting three hits that game, I didn't come through in extra innings. I struck out to open our half of the inning. We didn't manage a comeback. We dropped a game we had in our hands, 10–5. I just felt something went out of our team that night. I always look on that game as the game that led to our downfall—I just felt it.

WRAPPING IT UP

Amaro's choice of games is interesting. This loss to the Cardinals on September 9 antedated the calamitous 10-game skid by 11 games. The Phillies went 7–4 during the stretch in between the September 9 loss to St. Louis and the start of their 10-game losing streak. Many theories for the Phillies' collapse have been posited since 1964. Most concern Gene Mauch's meltdown of confidence, over-pitching Chris Short and Jim Bunning, team dissension, etc. Ruben cites a game 11 games prior to the team's 10-day losing skein as the day the music died in Philly. That's an insider's view that's intriguing.

"That 1964 season hurt for a long time," Amaro muses. "The 1980 team—when we won the championship—kind of erased some of those bad moments. Winning the World Series was like a dream. I never saw so many happy faces when our caravan was driving along on that parade route after the World Series. I can still see in my mind how happy my two sons, David and Ruben Jr. were. Of course, Ruben Jr. was a batboy back in those days. He was close to the team, so he felt the same sense of pride I did. I only wish he would have had the same opportunity in 1993 to play in the World Series when he was a player on that great team."

CHAPTER 21

RUBEN AMARO JR.

"I was part of the '93 team. We could sit down and talk all day about the memorable games that season, but I didn't play that much," recalls Ruben Amaro Jr. "I came back here to Philly from California in 1992 and unexpectedly got the opportunity to play. Lenny Dykstra got hurt and I was sent in to replace him. I had some really good games that first week filling in for Lenny. In fact, I'd have to say the game I remember most—the game of my life—was one of the games that week. It was the game when I got my first start for the Phillies."

MEET RUBEN AMARO JR.

Ruben Amaro Jr. was born on Lincoln's Day, February 12, but May 1 would have suited him better. May 1 (or April 30, depending on which source you consult) is the date in 1883 when the Philadelphia Phillies were born and played their first National League game. His dad, Ruben Amaro Sr., was born in Veracruz, Mexico, and came to Philadelphia after playing part of the '58 season for St. Louis. He played for the Phillies from 1960 through 1965, so Ruben Jr. is a Phillie through and through.

Amaro Jr. starred at the Delaware Valley's Penn Charter High School (class of '83). He followed with a stellar college career at Stanford. The California Angels drafted him and he spent his first big-league year as a California Angel debuting on June 8, 1991, against the Detroit Tigers. After his rookie season, he became a principle in the "second" Von Hayes deal—the less celebrated deal that was three players short of the more celebrated original. The first Von Hayes deal in 1983 cost the Phillies five players to bring the slender outfielder to Philadelphia. Eight years later, the Phillies dealt Von away and got Kyle Abbott and Amaro Jr. in return.

Ruben first came up to the Phillies in 1993 but didn't see any ML action until the season was well underway.

"The Phils had some terrific outfielders in '93," Amaro Jr. points out.

The Phils had acquired Milt Thompson and Pete Incaviglia in the '92 off-season. The duo platooned with Wes Chamberlain and Jim Eisenreich to give the squad one of the strongest outfield contingents in the majors.

"When I did get called up to the parent team in '93, it was intense in that clubhouse," Amaro Jr. recalls. "These guys were bound and determined they were going to go all the way and they weren't going to let anything get in their way. The Phils had added a lot of seasoned veterans, who came here believing they could win—even though nobody else in baseball thought they could. That '93 squad had guys like Milt, Inky, Larry Andersen, and Danny Jackson and they all knew what it was going to take for that team to win. The day I arrived, LA (Larry Andersen) and Danny Jackson took me out to dinner. They told me I had to get with the program fast. I thought they were kidding—for about a minute. Then I saw they were dead serious. LA said, 'It's different here this year. We're in this thing to win and everybody in that clubhouse has got to have the same attitude.'

"Being a native Philadelphian, I was really excited about playing in front of the Philly crowd," Amaro relates. "Just being in the clubhouse in '93 was an experience that I could write a book about. The stories about that crew could fill an encyclopedia.

"I was just a kid, and believe me, it was intimidating walking into that '93 clubhouse as a virtual rookie. Those guys—Kruk, Daulton, Hollins, and that crew—were dead serious about baseball and winning. I had to learn how to act and gain their acceptance. Here's what that meant—I had to play my guts out every second of every game just like they did. When those guys figured that's the way you play the game, I was accepted."

Ruben Amaro Jr. starred at Stanford and in the majors before moving to the Phillies front office. *David Seelig/Getty Images*

Amaro Jr. started for a while on the '94 Phillies—he wasn't supposed to be a starter. Lenny Dykstra had the center field job nailed down. But Amaro was rushed into the breach when the Dude (or "Nails" as he was known more commonly in New York) went down with an injury. Ruben started off like a house afire. Later, he cooled off and eventually found himself in a reduced role.

He played a few more seasons. The Phillies' performance declined, as we're painfully aware, after the '93-season high. Amaro was shipped off to the Cleveland Indians in 1995, where he once again was a member of the League Championship team. After a single season in Cleveland, he returned to Philly. He played for his native town for the next three seasons before deciding to hang it up. His final appearance for the Phillies was September 27, 1998. Afterward, he remained with the Phillies, working more on the business side of the house. He's currently the club's general manager.

SETTING THE STAGE

The Phillies were gung-ho going into the '92 season. The nucleus of the '93 pennant winners was in place. And even though the '91 Philly edition had finished last, they displayed encouraging promise—even flashes of brilliance like a 13-game win streak. Going into '92, the entire city was behind the Phillies.

"Lenny got hit," Curt Schilling recalls. "It happened on Lenny's first at-bat in the home opener. You could feel the whole stadium deflate. Actually, it was more than the stadium that deflated—it was the season."

Schilling is correct. In front of a packed, hopeful hometown crowd, Lenny Dykstra stepped in to face the Cubs' Greg Maddux to open the home half of the first inning. Maddux unleashed an inside pitch that sent Dykstra sprawling. The ball hit the Dude's hand and broke it. On one pitch, the Phillies lost their sparkplug and marquee player. They also lost their steam.

"I was sent in to replace Lenny," Amaro Jr. recollects. "I forget whether I went in right away or later in the game. I know I had one at-bat in the opener and didn't get a hit."

The next day, Amaro Jr. filled in for Lenny Dykstra in the Dude's centerfield slot. His start was a surprise to him. He would be going up against Cubs' pitcher Danny Jackson as the Phillies tried to avenge

THE GAME OF MY LIFE
APRIL 8, 1992
BY RUBEN AMARO JR.

It wasn't that bad a day weather-wise, just chilly. I think the chill kept some people out of the stands, and so did the disappointment of losing the opener the day before (attendance was only 16,328 for the second game). Tommy Greene took the hill for us. I wasn't certain I was going to play that day. When I came to the park, I saw that Jim Fregosi (manager) penciled me into the starting lineup and I got mentally prepared.

The Cubs had a big first inning. I think Ryne Sandberg hit a homer (that's correct: Sandberg clubbed a three-run homer with Sammy Sosa and Shawon Dunston on base). The point is, things didn't start very positively for us. We were down 3–0 before we got to the plate.

I led off and got plunked (for the second straight day, Cub pitchers plunked the first Philly batter). I think I scored—it was a small-ball score. We only had one hit along with a couple of groundouts that let me cross the plate. Tommy Greene settled down after his first-inning jitters. From that point on, we just kept coming back.

We were still down the next time I came up, but I was seeing the ball real well and Danny got one middle in, and I drove it into left field for a double. I ended up scoring again on a couple groundouts. The guys on that team in the early nineties—Hollins, Kruk, Daulton—knew how to play the game. When we got runners in scoring positions, guys knew how to move them around. They cut back on their swings, took pitches, worked the pitcher—and put runs on the board.

We started to get to Danny as the game moved along. The next time I came up, he gave me another one to hit and I drove it into left for another double and an RBI. We had a pretty big inning and took the lead for good.

Next time I came up, they had replaced Jackson. I guess I was just seeing the ball real well that day. The new pitcher got one middle in and I put it out in left-center. That's one of the biggest thrills I ever had. That was my first homer in the majors and I was fortunate enough to hit it in front of my hometown crowd. I had some sort of power surge that year. I hit seven homers in 1992, which was the most I ever hit (it accounted for approximately half of his career homers—he hit 16 homers in the pros).

I made an out in my last at-bat, but we got our first win of the season pretty convincingly (final score: Phillies 11 – Cubs 3). It was very satisfying to return to Philly and contribute so much to the first win of the season.

WRAPPING IT UP

"I had a tremendous week after that game," Amaro Jr. recalls. "I had a few homers and doubles and two-hit games. At the end of the week, I was on the leader board in a number of different offensive categories. Of course, that spree ended. I came back down to earth after that. But that week turned out to be quite a ride."

Amaro Jr. made more plate appearances in 1992 than in any other season in his major league career. By season's end, he had clubbed 15 doubles and seven home runs while scoring 43 runs.

CHAPTER 22

RANDY READY

"I gave it some thought and I have to say the game of my life was the game when I participated in the triple play," says Randy Ready. "I'd have to rate that incredible comeback against the Dodgers in LA right up there with it though. I don't know if you remember that game, but we were down 11–3 going into the ninth inning (August 21, 1990). That was the night Lasorda (Dodger manager Tommy Lasorda) was throwing things out of the dugout he was so steamed.

"I'll tell you a little about that game too," continues Ready. "We were in fourth place and pretty much out of the race (Nick Leyva's Phillies were 13 games behind at that late juncture). The Dodgers were fighting it out (Los Angeles was in second place at the time). Jason Grimsley started for us. We were tied for the first few innings. We fell a few runs behind after that.

"Then in the fifth the flood gates opened. L.A. scored a bunch of runs (eight) in one inning and jumped out 11–1. It looked like 'game over.' We scored a couple in the eighth (on Von Hayes' two-run double), but we went into the ninth behind 11–3. We started the inning with a few singles. They made an error and the game started to get interesting. Then Krukker pinch hits for Roger McDowell and slams a three-run homer to tie the game. Rod Booker got a hit and stole second and Carmelo Martinez knocked him in to go ahead. Don Carman came on in the bottom half of the inning and got the save.

"I remember that game so well, but I didn't get in the game. So I'll go with the triple play. That game I *was* in and participating in a triple play was something special."

MEET RANDY READY

"Krukker and I were both in San Diego when we got the call to go to Philly," says Randy Max Ready. "We were excited. I had always heard about the fans at Philly—how demanding they were and how tough they could be if they ever got on your case—that didn't bother me. I played the game all-out so I wasn't worried—neither was Kruk. I loved my years in Philly. Unfortunately I missed the '93 season. I was sent to Oakland in '92, but I could see they had a good nucleus of guys who hustled and busted their butts. I would like to have been part of that 1993 team.

"I was in Montreal at the time," he continues. "And I think most of the players in the league wanted to be in Philly. They could see how much fun those guys were having and how intensely they played as a team. They could see how that team bonded to win. Amazingly, I did make it back to the Phils the year after they won the pennant, but the team wasn't the same. We had too many serious injuries we couldn't overcome. Tommy Greene was hurt and lost for the season. Kruk had the bout with cancer. The Dude (Lenny Dykstra) was hurt. He played so hard in '93 and never got back to that same level because of his bad back.

"I've lived all over the country because of all the teams I've played for. But I enjoyed the Philly area. My whole family did. We lived in lots of different areas in the Delaware Valley like Main Line, center city, and Jersey. Philly's a great town and the fans are terrific. I made lots of good friends there. It would be great to have the opportunity some day to come back and manage or coach some day."

SETTING THE STAGE

The Phillies were off to another bad start. With only 18 games under their belt in the early stages of the 1991 campaign, they already had twice as many losses as wins (6–12). They were foundering six games off the 12–6 pace-setting Pirates.

The Fightins' opponents on April 28, 1991, were the San Diego Padres, who had jumped out to a promising 11–7 start. The Pads

---

Randy Ready , a well-trained veteran, participated in a rare triple play as a Phillie. *Ronald C. Modra/Sports Imagery/Getty Images*

were leading the pack in the NL West. On this day, they sent Eric Nolte to the mound to face the Phillies' Jason Grimsley.

"With Tony Gwynn, Fred McGriff, and Jack Clarke, the Padres had some pop in the middle of their lineup," explains Ready. "They were contenders that year. We were too. We had good talent with Dykstra, Von Hayes, Dale Murphy, Kruk, Charley Hayes and Daulton. Dutch was a guy we just knew was going to bust out with a big season soon and we were hoping 1992 was the season. The problem was, we didn't start out playing good ball. But this was a Sunday game at the Vet. We always seemed to play well on Sundays. For Kruk and me, any game against San Diego always gave us a little something extra since we had both come to Philly from San Diego. We both knew a little about their pitcher Eric Nolte too. Eric was with the Pads when Krukker and I were there."

THE GAME OF MY LIFE
APRIL 28, 1991
BY RANDY READY

I was starting at second base in place of Mickey Morandini, who made an unassisted triple play one season later. The game didn't start out so promising. The Padres started off the first inning with a walk. Then Paul Faries stole second. Next, our pitcher Jason Grimsley walked Tony Fernandez, their shortstop. Tony played with the Pads a couple of seasons after several great years with the Blue Jays. Fernandez went on to rejoin the Blue Jays in 1993 and square off against the Phils' "More Than Beards, Bellies, and Biceps" team in the '93 World Series. Then Tony Gwynn lined one my way. I grabbed it and tagged second. Fernandez, running from first, was only a couple of feet away from me on second base. Tony had stopped dead, knowing he was a dead duck. He could never have made it back to first base in time. I didn't tag him. I just tossed the ball over to Ricky Jordan at first for the third out.

I ran into the dugout—of course the fans were going wild. How often do you see a triple play? Vuke yelled at me, "Hey Spikey (Spike was my nickname) why didn't you tag Fernandez?"

Honest, I wasn't even thinking of anything like an unassisted triple play. My instincts told me to throw the ball to first—that's what I did. It never crossed my mind about how special a triple play was, let alone how rare an unassisted triple play was. So here's the way I look at it, I loved the glove I was using at the time. If I had made that play unassisted, they would have taken my glove away from me and sent it up to the Hall of Fame. I didn't want to lose that glove. Yeah, right—that's okay, my name is mentioned in the Hall of Fame a few other places anyway.

After the Padres went down in their half of the first inning, we answered with a big inning in our half. Dykstra started us off with a walk and a steal. When the inning was done, we had scored a bunch (five runs) and I played a part in it. I hit a single and drove in the second run. I was batting fifth in the order that day. A few batters after me, Charley Hayes hit a three-run homer.

The following inning we scored another three runs. I wasn't successful that time around—I grounded out. That inning, we scored by bunching a lot of singles and doubles. We ended up knocking Eric Nolte out of the game. After a few scoreless innings, I think we scored again (the Phillies added one on Dickie Thon's round-tripper) before the Padres finally got on the board (with Jack Clarke's two-run blast in the seventh).

WRAPPING IT UP

After the game, Phillies pitcher Jason Grimsley said, "It's a dream. The triple play was the whole game. Getting Tony Gwynn like that after two walks was terrific. That's a once in a lifetime thing."

Grimsley (1–3 at that point in the season) allowed three hits in seven innings, struck out seven and walked six, giving him 23 walks in 25⅓ innings. Tommy Greene finished the contest with hitless relief.

"Jason's right," says Fregosi, Phillies manager after the game. "The triple play turned the whole thing around. Grimsley was struggling early, but he had great stuff and threw the ball extremely well after that triple play gave us the lift."

Grimsley threw a wild pitch in the game. In fact, it was the ninth consecutive appearance in which he tossed a wild one. His inerrancy set a major league record and upped his total to 10 in the 18-game season. Jaime Cocanower of Milwaukee held the previous dubious record.

CHAPTER 23

WAYNE TWITCHELL

"I'll really throw you with my answer," says Wayne Twitchell. "The game of my life was a game I didn't even play in! Regardless, the most exciting game I ever saw was the wild one in Chicago in 1976 when we fell behind the Cubs 13–2 and came back for a win. I watched that whole thriller from the bench and never enjoyed a game as much as I did that one. If you ask me what game I remember most that I actually played in, well, that would be the game we clinched the division in '76. We were playing up in Montreal and I got to pitch in that game in relief. However my point is, I was a Phillie. I loved the team and loved the city, so the game of my life that I'd like to talk about is that game against the Cubs. We, the Phillies, came of age that day."

MEET WAYNE TWITCHELL

Wayne Lee Twitchell started his Phillies career slowly with a 1–0 record (in only 16 innings pitched) in 1971.

"One of my biggest thrills when I came to the Phillies was getting to meet Robin Roberts," Twitchell reflects. "Robbie came into the clubhouse one day shortly after I joined the team and I think I went speechless. I mean, literally speechless. I idolized Robin Roberts so much as a kid."

The following year, used chiefly in relief, Twitch pitched in 49 games but made only 15 starts in fashioning a 5–9 record and 3.59 ERA. In 1973 however, elevated to starting full time, he came on like a house afire. Each of four Phillies starters (Ken Brett, Steve Carlton, and Jim Lonborg) chipped in with 13 wins. All four shared the honor for most wins on the team (Dick Ruthven, the other starter, was 6–9). Of the quartet, Ken Brett's and Twitch's win-loss percentage (.591) led the Phillies staff. However, Twitch's 2.50 ERA led Brett and all other staff-mates (including future Hall of Famer Carlton) by a mile.

Twitch's dominance that year wasn't limited to the Phillies' staff. He finished third in ERA among NL hurlers. His five shutouts led the Philly squad but also ranked third among all NL peers. His 6.93 hits allowed per nine innings pitched ranked third, his 6.81 strikeouts per nine innings pitched was sixth best in the NL, and his 153 adjusted ERA was second best in the NL. Twitch's excellence that year earned him the Phillies' only All-Star berth.

"What a thrill that was," Twitch reminisces. "You know where I found out I was selected to the All-Star squad? I was at Camp Drum for my two-week summer camp with my Reserve Unit. I got a call from Paul Owens. I was a Track Commander in a Philly unit that I had transferred into when I was traded to the Phils. I had been a drill instructor in the Oregon unit I left. Summer camps there were more intense. We used to be assigned to Fort Lewis for two weeks to fill in for the regular army-drill instructors. That was a tough transition, going from baseball to a real army mentality. It's funny we're talking about this today. An old friend just sent me a photo of me throwing the ball around at Camp Drum in '73. That's where I prepared for the All-Star game!

"The All Star game itself was great," continues Twitch. "I was surrounded by amazing talent. I got to pitch too."

He pitched a scoreless sixth inning as the Nationals crushed the American League 7–1 in the 44th edition of the mid-summer classic. Meanwhile ex-Phillie Rick Wise started for the Nationals and got the win.

"Bobby Bonds won the MVP that game," says Twitch. "Bobby was such a nice guy, but his son sure is having his problems."

Tragedy struck a few months after the All Star contest.

"Unfortunately," Twitch reflects, "We played a late-season game in Chicago that derailed my career. Billy Williams, the all-time great Cub, hit a ball to the right side of the mound. Our first baseman

---

Wayne Twitchell, an All-Star hurler for the Phils in 1973, learned of his selection at Summer Camp in Fort Drum. *MLB Photos via Getty Images*

fielded it—I covered the bag. His throw led me to the runner's side of the bag and Billy slid into me and knocked my knee out from under me. I underwent a six-hour operation where they removed the entire ACL. I was never the same after that. But I never use that incident as an excuse. I just couldn't plant my leg properly after that so it altered my delivery."

In 1974, his record slumped to 6–9 and his ERA more than doubled, shooting up from 2.50 to 5.21.

"That was a special year for Hank Aaron so I gave up some homers to him," Twitch chuckles. "It was the year Hank passed Babe Ruth for most career homers. Aaron was such a nice guy. I got to know him a little in those years and was really impressed. Hank was soft-spoken and talented. He was also a terrific team player. The guy played the game the way it's meant to be played. I remember a game when I served him up a pitch that was definitely *not* in the location I wanted—not for Hank Aaron. But Hank didn't swing for the fences. The Braves needed a run. They had a man on second. So, Hank hit the pitch to the right side to move the runner up. That's the kind of player Hank was. Most guys only worry about their stats so they can negotiate salary more effectively. That's a reason why I admired Paul Owens in Philadelphia. The Pope (as Owens was known) knew the game. I saw him give guys who batted .270 higher salaries than guys who hit .290 because the guys who hit .290 didn't add as much value to the team. They didn't move runners, didn't lay bunts down when the situation called for it, and didn't do the little things that win games and pennants over a long season."

Twitch got only two starts in 1976 when his won-lost log sparkled at 3–1. Meanwhile, his ERA dropped to a career-best 1.75. For his career, Wayne's ERA wound up on the wrong side of 4.00 a few seasons, but he finished his career with an impressive 3.98 lifetime ERA.

Wayne was dealt to Montreal along with Tim Blackwell on June 15, 1977 for Barry Foote and Dan Warthen. For the Canadians, Twitch was a full-time starter. He went 6–5 with a 3.80 ERA. The following year however, despite a 3.54 ERA, his record tumbled to 4-12.

"I don't think I had the same stuff I had years earlier," Twitch confesses. "Willie Stargell hit a long, long home run off me, I remember. I think someone measured it and said it would have gone 534 feet or so. When I got back to Philly, I was talking in the outfield with Jim Bunning. Jim said, 'When they start hitting them that far, you have to start thinking about doing something else.'

"I'll tell you another thing about Stargell," Twitch continues. "When I was pitching for Montreal, they had a pool in the right-field area. Well, they used to go to the pool and make all the kids get out when Stargell took batting practice. That's some kind of respect.

"Those seventies Pirate teams could hit. I remember some statistic at the time that every Pirate in the lineup hit over .300 every time Steve Blass was on the hill. I think they did the same thing to me when I was on the hill against them. Al Downing had a quote after a game when Stargell had beaten him. The announcer asked Downing why he hadn't pitched around Willie. Downing answered, 'Why would I pitch around somebody to get to a .300 hitter!'"

Twitchell called it quits in 1979 and went into the real-estate business, where he has remained for 25 years.

"In 1992, I expanded into a pretty big operation," he shares. "I had 12 employees, but I got out of that situation. Now, I just do the business on my own. For the past 14 years, I volunteered as the official pitching coach for one of our high school teams in Portland, Oregon. Then the year after I stopped, when I decided it was time to let someone else do the job, they went to the state finals!"

"I think the last time I might have been to Philly was the Final Ceremonies at the Vet," Twitch concludes. "Gene Garber and I were approached by Chase Utley. Chase asked us what we would have done differently if we were given a second chance. Without hesitation, Gene responded, 'Enjoy the experience.' I concurred. It appears to me that Chase Utley has taken those words to heart. His desire and effort make me proud of the fact that I once wore the same uniform."

SETTING THE STAGE

"We weren't going very well at the beginning of 1976," Twitch offers. "The people in Philly were already getting down on us. We had talent on that team, but we didn't get out of the blocks too well."

The Phillies finished in second place in 1975, but at this point in the '76 season, they were 2–3 and in fourth place. In '75, they had placed an unprecedented four guys on the All-Star team (Larry Bowa, Dave Cash, Greg Luzinski, and Tug McGraw). Philadelphia fans, ever cautious after 1964, weren't fully sure their hometown heroes were for real.

On April 17, 1976, the Phillies were in Chicago. The Windy City was not, according to 1975 statistics, a propitious place for the

Phillies to turn their fortunes around. They had posted their worst head-to-head 1975 record against the Cubbies going a horrific 6–12 (.333). Other than Chicago, the only other two teams who had bested the Phillies in the '75 season series were the Dodgers and the Reds (does that surprise anyone? This was the era of the 'Big Red Machine'). In each case the season series was close, 5–7. The Cubs indeed seemed to have the Phillies' number.

THE GAME OF MY LIFE
APRIL 17, 1976
BY WAYNE TWITCHELL

The wind was blowing a ton that day—hey, it was Wrigley Field. We had just come off a loss at Montreal on Thursday and we were below .500. We weren't happy, our fans weren't happy. We went into that season with great expectations but those expectations weren't panning out so far. We had Steve Carlton on the mound and we always thought we were going to win behind him. We didn't start out too bad. I don't think either the Cubs or us scored in the first inning. Then in the second, Garry Maddox, who wound up having a big day, homered and we jumped ahead, but not for long. The Cubs came back like crazy and scored a bunch (the Cubs scored a touchdown and PAT in the bottom of the second, zooming out to a 7–1 lead). They knocked Lefty (Carlton) out and Ron Schueler took the mound. Next inning, the Cubs tagged Ron for a bunch more (the Cubs upped their advantage to 12–1 after three innings). We got one run back (on a Dave Cash RBI) in the top of the fourth, but the Cubs countered with another run (a Rick Monday solo blast).

There we were, down 13–2 at Wrigley. Things didn't look good, but then we didn't know this was a game that, years later, *Sports Illustrated* would pick as one of the 'ten games of the decade you wish you had seen.' Well, I'm glad I saw it. This was the classic game that proves the old Yogi Berra statement that "It ain't over till it's over."

We started to fight back.

In the top of the fifth, Mike Schmidt hit his first home run. That got us a couple more (Cubs 13 – Phillies 4). Believe it or not, we went quiet for a couple of innings after that. Then in the seventh, we had a big inning. Schmidt slammed his second straight homer and we cut the Cub lead to 13–7.

In the eighth, we kept it up. Schmidt blasted another one, his third straight homer, and we finished the inning down by only a run 13–12. Then in the ninth, Boonie (catcher Bob Boone) who had a big day too, as did Garry Maddox, led off the inning with a homer to tie the game. We followed with a few hits until Jay Johnstone bunted to score Bowa. That put us ahead. We went into the bottom of the ninth leading 17–15. It looked like we had the game in hand.

However, the Cubs came back and scored two to tie us (Tug McGraw could not preserve the lead as seventies' Phillies nemesis Steve Swisher plated two on his RBI single). But we weren't done— nor were the Cubs. In our half of the tenth, Schmidtty slammed his fourth straight homer to put us up by two. Dave Cash added an insurance run with a sacrifice fly. That made it 18–15 with the Cubs coming to bat. I think we had Tommy Underwood on the mound that inning, and the Cubs got one back to keep things exciting. But that was it. We won 18–16 in the tenth.

I think that was the day—that was the spark that set our team on fire. It might have been during the preseason that year or maybe it was the year before that Dave Cash started a team slogan, 'Yes we can!' Well, that day at Wrigley, our team finally realized Dave's saying was true—we really can!

WRAPPING IT UP

The "yes we can" crew did take off after that. The next day, Larry Christiansen again topped the Cubs. Two days later, Jim (Kitty) Kaat added a digit to the win column and two days hence, Tommy Underwood notched another. All of a sudden, the Phillies were 5–3 and in second place behind the Pirates.

On the wings of their incredible April 17 triumph at Wrigley, Philadelphia finished April 8–6. They went an astounding 22–5 for May, outscoring their opponents 150 runs to 70—and the Fightins went on to 101 wins to set a franchise record. Nonetheless, the Phillies' problems with the Cubs lingered. Philadelphia managed to take the '76 head-to-head series (10–8) with the Cubs, but again, they posted better records against every other team save two.

CHAPTER 24

DAVE RAYMOND

PHILLIE PHANATIC I

"It's hard to pick," says Dave Raymond, speaking of the game of his life. "I wound up being the Phillie Phanatic at a young age. I had just finished a summer of being a Phillie intern and, next season, I ended up being the original Phillie Phanatic. I got to live every man's dream. I had access to the guys out on the field. I got to see them every day and know them as friends. But that comfort level took a little period of adjustment. By the time 1980 rolled around, I was comfortable being around all those guys. It was kind of an amazing ride. The Phillies ballplayers were my sport heroes just a few years before. Now, by 1980, they were more like friends.

"When the 1980 World Series rolled around, I think that was the pinnacle. That was as good as it gets. I watched this team battle every year, fall a little short and come back for more the next year. They never lost faith and neither did I. I was fortunate enough to be in Houston for that entire series of remarkable games we played in the NLCS. And in answer to your question: 'What was the game of my life?' I'd have to say it was game five of the Houston National League Championship Series. You've probably heard the same thing from several guys you've talked to for this book. But it simply was the greatest game for any dyed-in-the-wool Phillies fan—That's the game I'll never forget."

MEET DAVE RAYMOND

"I was the perfect guy for the Phillie Phanatic job," Raymond reflects. "I don't know if that's a good thing or a bad thing. But I loved my Phanatic days."

Raymond grew up in a sport family. His dad, Tubby, coached the Delaware Blue Hens to over 300 wins.

"When I was a kid, I used to idolize the Delaware football player," says Raymond. "My dad was the coach so I was always at practices as a kid. When I actually played for Delaware, it was like a dream come true."

In his collegiate days, Dave was a punter for the Blue Hen squad. In the summer between his junior and senior years, he accepted a job as an intern with the Philadelphia Phillies.

"What a great job!" Raymond affirms looking back. "I quickly got to feel a part of the organization. In fact, Ed Wade, the same Ed Wade that eventually became the general manager, was an intern with me. We played a little two-on-two and three-on-three basketball that summer—interns versus the 'regular' members of the Phillies organization. We played about every week against David Montgomery (general partner, president and CEO) and Richard Deats (vice president of Phillies Enterprises). Those guys decided to put the two interns against each other to employ a little divide-and-conquer strategy. They kept telling me all week that Ed Wade was complaining that I shoot too much. Meanwhile, they told Ed the same thing about me. Sure enough, we started feuding with each other in the next game. I still don't think Montgomery won. Yeah, they were great days that summer."

Dave went back to Delaware for his final season, content that his Phillies days were now in his rear-view mirror.

"Then one day in college, I get a phone call from Frank Sullivan (the Phillies' promotions director)," continues Raymond. "Frank says, 'I have an offer for you.' Frank no sooner finishes saying that when Chrissy Long, another person in promotions, hops on the phone and blurts, 'Don't do it, Dave!' They were calling to offer me a shot at the Phillie Phanatic job. They had to explain what it was of course. And then I had to think about it."

Dave Raymond, the original Phillie Phanatic, learned a lot of his non-verbal communication skills from his mother, who was deaf.

"My fraternity brothers weren't encouraging," explains Raymond. "'Those Philly fans will be hanging you in effigy—and that's when the Phillies win!' I was initially hesitant to discuss the offer with my parents. I thought they'd nix it as an unwise use of a college degree. But they surprised me. They were all for it. Eventually I figured, 'Why not give it a try?' The only time I had ever been a mascot before was at the opening of a Grant's store. I went with my instincts and accepted the offer. It was one of the best choices of my life."

On April 25, 1978, the Philly fans were introduced to the Phillie Phanatic for the first time. Since then, the Phanatic has grown to be an institution on the local sport scene.

"I attribute some of my ability to communicate in mime to my mom," Raymond explains.

His mom, Suzanne Raymond, was deaf and very active in the deaf community. She was certified in sign language and a teacher at the Sterck School for Deaf Children in Newark, Delaware. She was once honored as Delaware's Deaf Person of the Year.

Raymond turned the mascot gig over to Tom Burgoyne after the 1993 season. He started his own business, Raymond Entertainment Group, which does everything conceivable in the mascot world—from concept to creation, to animation to branding, to whatever. His customer list includes clients all over North America. Though donning the big green costume is now a thing of the past, Raymond continues being a Phillie fanatic, in or out of costume.

SETTING THE STAGE

"As the Phanatic, of course, I was always around the ballplayers," says Raymond. "Getting comfortable with that was a real transition—I mean, these guys were my heroes. I was intimidated for a long while. I didn't dare even talk to them unless they talked to me. But as I got to know them and see them day after day, I grew more comfortable. It was a thrill to find myself being accepted. Guys like Pete Rose would see me, walk over and ask, 'How's it going, Dave?' It felt strange at first.

"By 1980, I felt close to these guys," he continues. "I also came to a good realization of how different pro ball is than high school and even college ball. I always think of Garry Maddox in that light. Gary and I became good friends. He's just a tremendous guy and one of the best ballplayers we ever had in town. When he missed that fly ball in the playoff game against Los Angeles, I think I took it as hard as Gary did. It was just one of those flukes. When you're so good at something you never even have to think about it. That's what catching a ball was to Garry. Well, I grew to understand what the pain of carrying an incident like that is. The difference between pro ball and any other level is that, in pro ball, those things never go away. They stay with you forever. I saw how that hurts and I was so glad when the Phillies and guys like Garry got a shot at redemption in the Houston series.

"I was personally fortunate in that series," he explains. "I was invited to perform before the games in Houston, so I accompanied the team. I would go out onto the field during practice and orchestrate boos. I'd pit one section of the stadium against another to see who could boo me the loudest. I ad-libbed some routines with the Houston players too. I always had fun with that Houston team when they came to Philly. Guys like Enos Cabell were great guys who interacted well with the Phanatic. They would stage stunts. For example, Enos would bend down behind me while another Houston guy would push me backward. I'd tumble head over heels over Enos. The Astros were always up for doing those types of things. I think I stomped on the Houston logo too. I'd do things like that and they got a kick out of it.

"At the end of my routine, a couple of Texas State policemen would come out and arrest me and haul me off the field in handcuffs. Those guys were serious! I talked to them before I went out to the field and orchestrated the whole thing, but they were dead serious when they did it. Fortunately, they didn't go all the way through with the routine and actually jail me.

"The Houston ownership was great to me. They told me that, as long as I was there, I should be able to sit on the bench when my routine was over. They got me a batboy's uniform and I sat on the bench in the thick of all the action for all three games. And these were maybe the most exciting games the Phillies ever played.

"It was a best-of-five series in those days. We split the first two games at the Vet. Next, we went to Houston for the remainder of the series. The Astros beat us 1–0 in 11 innings, followed by a 5–3 ten-inning Phillies win. That brought up the deciding game with Marty Bystrom, a rookie, going against Nolan Ryan in Houston."

THE GAME OF MY LIFE
OCTOBER 12, 1980
BY DAVE RAYMOND

The Astrodome was unbelievably loud. It was amazing being on the field. I could hear so much—so many of the things fans aren't privy to hearing. One time, Pete Rose hit a foul into the stands. The fans went wild. Pete yelled over to our dugout, 'It's a football town. They don't understand baseball!' Little things like that were awesome, being so close to the action.

It was amazing to feel the intensity and emotion on the bench first-hand. We had never been able to pull off an NLCS title in the late seventies. The guys on the team knew this might be their one last chance. I could feel they were *not* going to let that chance slip away.

The emotion level of the game was so high; the details are almost a blur. I know Manny Trillo had an amazing day. I know we fell behind in the first. We did *not* want to give Nolan Ryan any advantage to work with and we came back with a couple of runs in the second to go ahead.

Houston had a huge seventh inning. Art Howe hit a big triple and we went into the eighth leading 5–2. I found out after the game that Nolan Ryan had some unbelievable stats about winning when he was leading a game in the eighth. But the Phillies answered right back. Manny Trillo got the big hit for us—a triple that put us out front. We came out of the inning leading 7–5. But doesn't Houston come back to score two in their half of the eighth to tie.

The game went into extra innings. In the top of the tenth, Mike Schmidt struck out. But Del Unser doubled and Garry Maddox hit a double to drive in the game-winning run. I think I was happier for Garry than he was. That's what I mean—having been with those guys for so long and feeling so comfortable with them all, the whole atmosphere felt like family. I never felt better for anyone than I felt for Garry Maddox that day.

After the game, I ran on to the field with my batboy uniform. I ran into the locker room. I was one of the first ones in. There was all this champagne all over and I didn't know what to do. I hardly drank. I still don't. But this day was special and I started drinking. I drank way too much. I remember the Bull (Greg Luzinski) coming over to me at one point and grabbing me. 'You're not supposed to drink *that* stuff,' he was saying. He meant that I was drinking the cheap champagne they put in the locker room to shoot at everyone when the guys first get back into the clubhouse! I didn't know. I drank too much of the cheap stuff. I had a wicked headache the next day from that champagne, but it was worth it for that win.

WRAPPING IT UP

"We moved on to play Kansas City after winning the NLCS in Houston," continues Raymond. "I didn't perform there. I actually got a phone call from Mr. Kaufman, who owned the Royals at the time. He said I couldn't perform. It wasn't that he didn't like the Phanatic's act. It's just that he I didn't want the Royal fans to start asking for a mascot!"

The Phillies went onto World Series glory as every Philly schoolchild knows, and Raymond went on to 13 more years of bringing another fun dimension to a day at the park.

CHAPTER 25

TOM BURGOYNE

PHILLIE PHANATIC II

"I'd have to think for a week on that one!" says Tom Burgoyne.

One week later, same question: "So what was the game of your life?"

"I'd have to think for a week on that one!" he says

The author then convinced Tom that he had to choose the game of his life that very instant. The author had a deadline to meet and Burgoyne (the Phanatic) had a tendency to come up with a different favorite game-of-my-life every week.

Two minutes later. . . .

"Okay, since we talked about so many of my favorite games in our other books (Burgoyne and I co-authored *More Than Beards, Bellies, and Biceps, The Story of the 1993 Phillies and the Phillie Phanatic Too* and *Movin' On Up*), I'll pick a different game from any games that we wrote about previously," explains Burgoyne. "I've had some great moments, some amazing memories with people like Tommy Lasorda, Joe Carter, and Ozzie Smith. I've had some awesome memories when I wasn't the Phanatic too—especially during the '93 season. That year I was the back-up Phanatic. My other job was playing the music at the Vet, picking out songs like the Stones' 'Start Me Up' for The Dude, Lenny Dykstra. As for games, that 4:49 a.m. game is one that leaps to mind. But honestly, and this might be scary, it might show I'm getting sentimental in my old age.

"I think I'd have to pick the last game at the Vet. That was an amazing day. I never felt electricity like I felt in the park, even though the game itself was sort of secondary. So yeah, that's the game I'd pick as the game of my life."

MEET TOM BURGOYNE

"I was raised at the Vet," Tom Burgoyne admits. "My brothers and I used to head out there every chance we got. My dad took us one day to see the Chicken Man when San Diego was in town. When I saw Chicken Man as a kid, I thought he had the coolest 'job' in the world. I didn't think much about doing any mascot-ing until I got to St. Joe's Prep. I played in the band for a few years there. But when senior year rolled around, I decided to 'run' for the Hawk mascot position. At the Prep, the students vote for the Hawk mascot—being elected is a privilege and an honor. Well, I got picked to be the Hawk. I'll be honest. The Phillie Phanatic was my 'role model' of sorts when I became the Hawk. The Phillie Phanatic personality and style shaped my approach to being the Hawk. I didn't want to have the entire 'personality' of the Hawk restricted to doing the arm-flap thing (the Hawk mascot by tradition never stops flapping its 'wings' at an athletic contest). Of course I did flap my arms—I maintained the tradition. I just thought the Hawk had a lot more potential to entertain, and I felt that way from seeing what Dave Raymond had done with the Phillie Phanatic. I always thought, 'Now *there* is a mascot with personality.'"

Burgoyne answered a somewhat inscrutable 'Want Ad' that sparsely stated, "Mascot wanted." Not knowing who was looking for a mascot or what mascot they were looking for, he responded. Burgoyne unexpectedly found himself auditioning for the role of backup Phillie Phanatic (the full, hilarious "Phanatic audition story" can be found in *More Than Beards, Bellies and Biceps*). Suffice it to say, he got the job. Burgoyne backed up Dave Raymond, the original wearer of the green for the next few years. During that time, in addition to his Phanatic back-up role, he was involved in all kinds of Phillies projects, not the least of which was choosing and playing the music for each Phillie batter that stepped up to the plate.

Tom Burgoyne, the Phillie Phanatic's best friend, was voted top mascot in 2008 on Forbes.com. He regrets only not making any of the site's best-paid lists.

He did some stepping of his own in 1994 when he was named the official Phillie Phanatic after Dave Ramond left for greener (so to speak) pastures. Burgoyne had some big shoes to fill (literally—they're size 16s). Raymond had endowed a lifeless costume with a unique, wacky but lovable personality. Certainly, Raymond's task demanded creative thinking. However, Burgoyne as his successor confronted equally daunting challenges. He had to sustain and grow the mascot's persona and kept the Phanatic's act engaging, entertaining, and topical. In the hands of a lesser artist, the Phillie Phanatic could become stale and old. The fact that the Phanatic still reigns supreme in terms of recognition and popularity among all professional sport mascots, confirms Burgoyne's success. In the volatile, swirling maelstrom that is Major League Baseball, players and coaches come and go. They switch allegiances to other teams and other cities. The Phillie Phanatic, however, remains virtually the lone Phillies and Philly constant.

As mentioned above, the Phanatic has also proven himself a successful author. Meanwhile, he remains one of Philly's most sought-after celebrities logging over 500 appearances a year—either as the Phanatic or the "Phanatic's best friend."

SETTING THE STAGE

"The entire final year at the Vet was amazing," says Tom Burgoyne. "The excitement of moving to a new park the following year was awesome, but the buzz about the end of an era at the Vet just grew and grew all season long. After all those years of complaining about the Vet—hearing fans, commentators, and players calling it substandard, outdated, and obsolete (and those were the kindest descriptions)—everyone started to grow more and more nostalgic about the old place. And the Phils did the Vet proud with their incredible season-long tribute and memorial.

"My favorite part of the final year was the Countdown Clock, which hung prominently in the right-field corner on the fence," remembers Burgoyne. "All season long, night after night, I chauffeured a list of notables out there. Each 'dignitary' removed the number hanging on the clock and replaced it with the next lower number.

"Okay, it wasn't really a *clock*," he admits. "It was more like an Advent Calendar, but calling it a 'clock' worked for our fans. I had the privilege of taking people like Governor Rendel, Greg Luzinski, Jim Eisenreich, Tony Taylor, Willie 'the Phillie' Montanez, Bill Conlin, and Connie Mack's two daughters out there. I'll never forget Mike Krukow. Mike removed number 67 from the wall and put up a sign 'Get Well Tug' for Tug McGraw, who was fighting a life-and-death battle with cancer. I took Tug out there too—Tug and his little son Matthew. Some of those appearances had an almost eerie timing—particularly the guys who did the final 'Countdown Clock' visits on the closing weekend. Lefty Carlton took down number three and put up number two. Lefty happened to be number two on the all-time strikeout list at the time. Then Schmidty removed number two the following day on what happened to be his own birthday.

"When the final weekend came, the excitement and nostalgia were at a fever pitch. It might have been my greatest day ever at a ballpark. That's why that last game at the Vet was the game of my life."

THE GAME OF MY LIFE
SEPTEMBER 28, 2003
BY TOM BURGOYNE

The big day arrived. I've got to admit, I was swept up in the nostalgia. All the memories of the Vet that I had stored away, all the days and nights I had spent there, everything came back that final day. The amazing thing was, I could sense that everyone in the stadium shared those same sentiments—those same emotions. Every fan in the park felt like he or she was saying a final farewell to an old friend. As for the game itself, I don't remember much about it. We lost—enough said. We closed out all those fun years by losing to our old nemesis—the Braves. Chase Utley grounded out to end the game, end the era, and bring on the closing ceremonies—that's what the whole park was waiting for anyway.

I made up my mind to visit as many fans as I possibly could that day. I tried to get up to places in the stadium that I didn't visit too often because they were pretty inaccessible in this costume. I'm talking about the remote, tough-to-reach corners of the Vet—up around the 600 and 700 level. I walked around the entire park between the 500 and 600 level and it was awesome. I never expected the reception and enthusiasm I encountered. I was mobbed! The entire circuit around the Vet, I was greeted by fans running up to me. I doubt if I'll ever sense that kind of electricity again. Everyone was high-fiving and screaming.

Again, I give the Phillies credit. The organization had really thought this whole thing out. They added so many little touches to the festivities. Jerry Crawford umpired. Jerry is a native Philadelphian. His dad, Shag, had umpired the opening game at the Vet. The ground crew wore tuxedos. And of course, the golden-throated Harry Kalas emceed. Harry had emceed the opening ceremonies at the Vet all those years ago. In fact, the Vet's opening ceremonies were Harry the K's introduction to Phillie fans. Now here it was, all these years later and Harry had become a Philly institution in his own right.

I took Harry Kalas out in the sidecar that day to the Countdown Clock. Harry removed the final number, number one, as every Phillie fan knows, was the jersey number that Richie Ashburn wore. Whitey was Harry's old sidekick in and out of the booth for years. Harry blew a kiss skyward to Whitey.

The whole day was wall-to-wall nostalgia. I normally was allotted a minute and a half in the fifth inning to do my mid-game routine—this day was different. I danced to the entire song, "Let's Just Kiss and Say Goodbye" by the Manhattans. That was the theme for the entire day—no one was in a hurry. After the game and after the festivities even, no one wanted to leave. Everyone lingered, trying to stretch the day out as long as possible.

As for the postgame festivities, they were awesome. Once the game was over, Harry started things off by introducing the Phanatic. I waddled over to the dugout roof, my on-field 'office' for so many years, and danced to Donna Summer's "Last Dance." You know, the Phanatic doesn't always 'clear' things with the Phillies first, so I invited everyone to join me. I don't know how many people leaped up on the dugout roof to dance up a storm. I do know there were some structural considerations that I probably should have pre-considered, but the Phanatic doesn't always think things through completely.

Afterward, there was a year-by-year procession of ex-Phillies. They didn't announce the guys' names over the PA—they just showed their names on Phanavision. Some of the guys put on great shows. Bob Dernier slid into home. Steve Bedrosian did a snow angel on the mound—things like that. But the fact that the procession took place in silence, except for the fans cheers, added a special touch.

At the end, Tug reenacted the Willie Wilson strikeout that ended the '80s Series. Tug was the final "memory" of the three that were reenacted. Prior to Tug, Lefty (Carlton) had reenacted striking out his 3,000th batter and Schmidtty reenacted hitting his 500th homer. Harry made a slight faux pas on that one. As Schmidtty pantomimed his 500th home run trot, Harry announced it as his 548th homer. It didn't matter. Only the sentiment mattered.

It's still hard to believe that we lost Tug so quickly after that day. I was down in Florida a few months later at Spring Training with Tug. We were planning to resurrect the old "Irish Mike" Ryan routine to kick off the upcoming season. The Phanatic was going to drop a ball down from a helicopter and Tug would catch it, as Irish Mike had done years before. Do you know what Tug did in rehearsal? I dropped the ball and Tug caught it behind his back. Tug died only a short time later, but the fact that he could still catch a ball behind his back in his weakened physical condition was amazing.

Paul Owens was at the Final Ceremonies too, looking frail but happy. We lost Paul that off-season as well. Yeah, Tug and the Pope (as Owens was nicknamed)—two guys who had done so much to make the Phillies the powerhouse they were in the late seventies and early eighties. It seems tragic that neither one ever got to see the Phillies move into our super, new stadium.

When the festivities were over, Harry took the microphone and uttered the Vet's final words, "It's like a 3–1 pitch to Michael Jack or Jim Thome. It's a long drive. It's outta here. God bless you."

Everyone sort of milled around and took their time vacating the place. The people in the Phillies organization got together in the offices for a little celebration, once the place cleared. We kind of wandered down to the field for the last time and reminisced. It was a great day. I think Skip Denenberg, the unofficial songwriter for the Phillies and WIP, captured the sentiment best in the song he wrote especially for the Final Ceremonies, "We'll remember the way it used to make us feel. It was so much more than concrete and steel."

WRAPPING IT UP

On March 21, 2004, Veteran's Stadium was imploded to the ground. Crowds started forming near the old stadium at 4 a.m. By 5 a.m., news vans and more than 200 media types were swarming the terrain. The Phillies set up a hospitality tent serving coffee and doughnuts to the weary and bleary-eyed. Longtime Phillie PA man, Dan Baker, blasted out Vet trivia to the crowd, Mayor Street gave a speech, and Greg Luzinski (in a symbolic final "Bull Blast") pressed the ceremonial plunger on the ceremonial detonator. Seconds later, a series of deafening explosions circumnavigated the grand old lady of the seventies. Minutes later, Veterans Stadium belonged to the ages. Nothing but rubble remained of a site that had hosted World Series contests, NFL playoff games, three decades of home games for two professional sport franchises, and rock megastars like U2 and Paul McCartney. The Vet is dead. Long live the Vet.

CHAPTER 26

DON HASENMAYER

"I sure didn't get to play many major league games with the Phillies or anyone else," says Don Hasenmayer, "and those days were a long time ago now. But, sure, I remember my major league days—they were special. Anytime you have the good fortune to play baseball at the major league level, it's special. The games kind of blend at this point, since I wasn't a starting player. I only played partial games. I remember the first game I ever got in (on May 2, 1945). I was a pinch-runner against the Giants at the Polo Grounds. At that point, Freddie Fitzsimmons was the manager of the Phillies. He was replaced later in the season by Ben Chapman. It was a wild game. The Giants had a big lead (they were up 7–0), but we came back and almost won it (Giants 8 – Phils 7). The game that sticks out most was the day I hit a double down the right-field line at the Polo Grounds. It was the only extra-base hit of my major-league career."

MEET DON HASENMAYER

"I didn't have much of a major-league career, but I'm fortunate to have experienced a taste of it," says Don Hasenmayer. "I was a local kid, so I grew up as a Phillies fan—well, I was a fan of both the Phillies and the A's. I was only 18 when I first played for the Phils. Of course, it was war time and most of the players were away fighting the war. My time to serve came right after the season when I was called into active service. I served on the USS *Kearsarge*. It was the first carrier to pick up an astronaut in the water. The war ended by '45 and I was back at the Phils training camp in '46."

The Phillies trained in Miami in '46. They did their spring training in Wilmington from 1944–1945 after holding spring training in Hershey in '43. They chose the frigid northern climates for spring training because wartime restrictions on travel prohibited the average citizen—which baseball players of that era were considered—from traveling to "faraway" destinations like Florida. This bit of history underscores a foreign notion to modern administrations; namely that wartime sacrifice by citizenry at-large should be an accepted consequence of war.

"I came back from the war, went to spring training, and came up later in the season to the Phils," continues Hasenmayer. "Mostly I was used as a base runner. Our manager at the time was Ben Chapman. He was a real old-timer. He wouldn't use the young guys. He just didn't believe in using kids, but Chapman liked me. I know he has a bad reputation. He was the guy that gave Jackie Robinson so much trouble when he came up with the Dodgers. I think Ben was a southern guy and he was hard boiled (Chapman was born in Nashville, Tennessee). Still, for some reason he liked me. He'd send me in to run the bases for somebody and he'd tell me, 'When you get down to second, I don't want to see that guy standing.' I played hard and he liked that. I think if he had stayed in Philly, he would have brought me up, but he didn't. In '47, most of the regular guys came back from the war and I went down to the minors. I went to Terre Haute. I played third base and Willie 'Puddin Head' Jones played shortstop. We won the 3-I League title. Then we played a five-game series with Iowa. We lost two games then took a 500-mile trip in a hot school bus to Iowa and we got beat again. The ballfields there didn't look like the one in that *Field of Dreams* movie, I'll tell you that much. All we saw were cornfields 500 miles out and 500 miles back.

"In '48, I went to Wilmington, Delaware, and played on the same team with Robin Roberts—at least until August when he was called up. I hit well there, too—same as I did in Terre Haute. In '49 I went to Utica, which was the club that so many of the Whiz Kids had played on. Eddie Sawyer had just left when I got there in '48. He went to manage the Phillies. By the time I got to Utica, Richie Ashburn and Granny Hamner and all those guys were gone and we

Don Hasenmayer was a local kid who played briefly with the Phillies in the Forties. *Photo courtesy of Don Hasenmayer*

were only a so-so club. In 1950, I was only 23 and I was a player-manager for Vandergrift—a town near Pittsburgh.

"I hit .370 that year. I managed too," says Hasenmayer. "Can you imagine that? I was a 23-year-old kid, who had to pay all the kids on the team. We didn't have credit cards in those days. I paid them in cash for their meals and hotels and salaries. The deal was that we would be paid out of gate receipts, but the town couldn't support the team so the season ended early and abruptly.

"In 1950, I was at Fort Smith Virginia playing for a Red Sox farm team managed by Marty Marion—y'know who I roomed with? Jimmy Piersall! We had quite a time with Jimmy. We would have to stop him from chasing people up into the grandstands and things like that."

Fear Strikes Out is a 1957 movie recounting the Jimmy Piersall story—a battle with his mental illness. The movie cast a laughably uncoordinated Anthony Perkins as an unconvincing, Norman-Bates-if-he-pursued-baseball-instead-of-the-hospitality-industry-for-a-career, Jimmy Piersall with Karl Malden as his convincingly obnoxious domineering dad, John Piersall.

"In 1951, I was 24 years old," continued Hasenmayer. "I had the chance to play for Tampa Bay but I decided not to. Chapman was managing them. He went up to the majors and managed the Reds in '52. I think if I had played, he would have brought me along, but I'll never know. My wife and I decided to return to the Roslyn area and I'd get started in my father's plastering business (Hasenmayer and Sons).

"That's what I did with my life from 1952 on. I had a good life. I retired from plastering in '92. I still keep active. I cut the grass at the Fairways, the golf course near me, twice a week on Thursdays and Fridays. They're long days—nine, ten hours. My wife Terry and I still get out and around. We've been married 60 years now! We just went to San Francisco for our wedding anniversary. We're in good health, active, and life has been kind to us."

SETTING THE STAGE

The 1945 Phillies had finished dead last once again, logging a pathetic 46–108 record under manager Freddie Fitzsimmons and his midseason replacement, Ben Chapman. Of the future Whiz Kids, only catcher Andy Seminick was in place on the '45 edition of the club. In '46, Del Ennis joined him. His rookie-of-the-year level of production boosted the team a couple of notches both in the standings and league respect. Nonetheless, the Phillies and their fans had little hope for the season. Hasenmayer came up to the squad late in the season and got a few appearances in. Little did he know that these would be his final appearances on the big-league stage.

THE GAME OF MY LIFE
SEPTEMBER 28 1946
BY DON HASENMAYER

We were at the end of the season with only two games left to play. We didn't finish last. We had moved up to the top of the bottom half of the division but we were way out of the race (the Phillies were in fifth place out of eight teams and were 27 games behind). I got a rare chance to start.

The regular third baseman, Jim Tabor, was out of the lineup for some reason, so I played third base. I was batting fifth, right behind Del Ennis at cleanup. We fell behind pretty quick (after two innings, it was Giants 3, Phils 0; after three innings, Giants 6, Phils 2).

We were never in the game. But in my third at-bat, I hit one down the right-field line for a double. There weren't many people there in that huge place (the attendance was only 2,691) since both teams were out of contention—still, it was a thrill. I think that double was my only hit that day (Don was 1–4) and I did all right in the field (Don recorded five assists, but did have an error). We dropped the game, but I got a major league start and a double to boot.

WRAPPING IT UP

The next day, the Phillies went on to lose to the Giants again in the last game of the year. The Giants closed their season with a 12–10 advantage over the Phillies in head-to-head competition. The Phillies were the only team they topped in head-to-head play.

On that final day, Hasenmayer was the starting third basemen again. This time he took the collar in four at-bats as did most of his Phillie mates. Sheldon Jones of the Giants sent the Phillies into the off-season with a 3–1 loss. The attention of the fans in attendance was distant. Most watched the scoreboard for updates on the meaningful contest being waged cross-town. The St. Louis Browns and Brooklyn Dodgers were battling it out for the pennant at Ebbets Field.

As for the Phillies, another young hopeful started at shortstop, Granny Hamner. In '48, Hamner would start at second base with Putsy Caballero at third. By '49 the third baseman would be Puddin' Head Jones, Hasenmayer's old shortstop mate at Terre Haute. Puddin' Head, Ennis, Hamner, and others would become the nucleus of the 1950 Whiz Kids. Don Hasenmayer was so close to being right there with them.

CHAPTER 27

BOBBY SHANTZ

"I only played for the Phillies one season, and that was only for part of the year," says Bobby Shantz, pondering the game of his life as a Phillie. "Yeah, I know, but what a season, right? 1964. I was there for the whole sad ending. Personally, my most memorable games were in the early part of my career before I hurt my arm. I remember a big 14-inning game against the Yankees when I was with the A's. I pitched the entire game and won 2–1. Mickey Mantle hit a homer off me in the seventh to tie the game at one. Then we finally scored again in the top of the 14th. In the bottom half of the 14th, I got the first two Yankees out when up steps Mantle again. He hit one against the wall. Fortunately it stayed in the yard and I got the next batter, Hank Bauer, who was no pushover himself, for the third out. The whole game long, I think our manager, Jimmy Dykes, was trying to yank me out of the game. He kept running out to the mound, asking me if I wanted to keep pitching. I kept telling him, 'I sure do. I've been in the game this long. If anyone's going to lose it, I want it to be me.' That was a real memorable game."

(Author's Note: Bobby Shantz is perhaps the most humble athlete I ever met. The season he's referring to is 1952 when he won the American League MVP in the heyday of Mantle, Yogi Berra, Ted Williams, Whitey Ford, and other legends).

"Then there was the 1952 All-Star game in Philly," says Shantz. "Being a native Philadelphian, I was thrilled to play an All-Star game in front of the home crowd. And the city of Philadelphia had so many good pitchers that year. Robbie (Robin Roberts) won 28 that year and Curt Simmons won 14 with a great ERA. Curt had some injury problems as I remember or he'd have won lots more. All three of us were on the All-Star team. Curt and I were supposed to start against each other in sort of a hometown showdown, but I didn't get the start. Curt started for the Nationals. I got into the game in the fifth and struck out the side, one, two, three—Whitey Lockman, Jackie Robinson, and Stan Musial. The game was called after that inning because of rain so I didn't have a chance to go further. You know, one of the great legends in baseball has always been the 1934 All-Star game when Carl Hubbell struck out five future Hall of Famers in a row. It would have been nice to try to beat or repeat Hubbell's feat, but as it was, it was a thrill to have all my family and friends in the stands to see it (if you can believe it, 32,785 was the attendance at sold-out Connie Mack Stadium).

"As for my Phillies career, I'd have to say the day I beat Drysdale was the game of my life. I had a couple of good outings against the Dodgers that year. But this particular day I was really on. I felt good physically. I also felt I contributed a needed win to the team. This was an important game going down the stretch and I fulfilled a role that I wasn't supposed to fill to get that win—namely pitching in long relief. And of course beating Don Drysdale was nice. Drysdale was a tough competitor, so coming out on top against him any time was especially satisfying."

MEET BOBBY SHANTZ

Robert Clayton Shantz was born in Pottstown. In a two-team baseball city he grew up an A's fan.

"Most people in Philly were A's fans," Shantz recalls. "I was a bit young when the A's had their legendary teams of the late twenties and early thirties. Those guys were my heroes when I started playing baseball because guys like Foxx, Simmons, and Grove were still big stars. My dad used to take my brother Wilmer (who also played MLB) and me to Shibe Park to watch the A's—not the Phillies. When I got older things reversed. The Phillies got hot when the Whiz Kids came along. The city switched allegiance over to the Phillies and Philadelphia

Bobby Shantz won the MVP pitching for the Philadelphia A's, and did a yeoman's job in the '64 Phillies bullpen.

became a Phillies' city. That's when the A's moved out to Kansas City."

Shantz played at Pottstown High School. He wasn't a huge high school star, just a good ballplayer.

"I didn't pitch then," he points out. "I was only about 4'11" in high school. I didn't start to pitch until I played in semi-pro and sand-lot leagues. I pitched in the service too."

Naturally, Shantz's stellar diamond career post high school tops any of his alma mater's other alumni. Accordingly, Pottstown High is naming its new baseball park after Shantz—the guy who was shooed from the mound as a student because he was too small.

"The people at the high school called me the other day," Shantz continues. "They want me to come up for some kind of ceremony to dedicate the field. I told them I'll go if I don't have to give a speech. I can still run around the bases—at least I think I can. I'd rather do that than give a speech."

All his life, Bobby fought bias against his height, or lack thereof. He was so small the Armed Services rejected him during a world war.

"I went down to enlist and they turned me away because I didn't meet the minimum height requirement," Shantz chuckles. "I went back home and went again to the recruitment office several months later. I had grown an inch, so they enlisted me."

When Bobby returned from the service he played for several teams in the Philly area.

"I was playing in Souderton," reminisces Shantz. "Larry Glick was the manager of our team. We were in a semipro league. A guy named Bill Hockenberry is the one who, I guess you would say, dis-covered me. Harry O'Donnell was the scout for the Athletics that signed me. Besides Souderton, I played for the Holmesburg Ramblers and Forrest Hill in northeast Philly when I worked for the Disston Saw Works in the Northeast. I was playing in the northeast when the Phillies scouted me. Jocko Conlan was the Phillies' top scout. He came to watch me pitch. I didn't know he was in the stands until he came down to the field after the game.

"He told me I had a hell of a curve and a good arm but I was just too damn small. Well, four years later after I had that good 1952 sea-son, he sat next to me at a banquet. I'll be honest, I didn't recognize Jocko. I don't think I ever saw him after he scouted me in that game. Finally, he said to me, 'You know, Shantzy, I didn't make many mis-takes but I sure did with you.' I thought that was really nice of him.

He was sincere. I agree with him. I don't think he made many mistakes. He signed a lot of talent.

"People nowadays don't realize it, but when the Carpenter family bought the Phillies in the mid-forties, they really opened their wallets wide to sign some good talent. They signed Robin Roberts, Curt Simmons, Granny Hamner, Richie Ashburn, and Del Ennis—all that talent on the Whiz Kids. If I was the one that got away, I'm honored because the guys he signed were terrific ballplayers."

"You know, I ended up pitching against Curt Simmons in Egypt, Pennsylvania," continues Shantz with a smile. "That was Curt's hometown. My team had won the East Penn League and the Phils were wooing Curt at that point. Lots of teams were. Anyway, we played a big exhibition game and I got the win. Curt still laughs about that when we play golf at his place."

Curt's place is in Horsham. Simmons and Robin Roberts, his fifties mate, have owned the golf course there for years. Today, Shantz is on those links as often as his legs can carry him, which is daily.

"I'm an eight-handicap," reveals Shantz. "I still golf under my age (I'm 82). I still walk the course. My wife is after me all the time to take a cart, but I haven't given in yet. I made up my mind after working 22 years at the Dairy Barn that I was going to play golf the rest of my life and that's what I've done."

The Dairy Barn was Shantz's business on Route 202 in Chalfont. He, his brother and a few other ex-A's and ex-Yankee chums bought a bowling alley and dairy bar in the mid-sixties. The Dairy Bar became his second career—a career he didn't relish as much as his first career.

In his first career, Shantz attained some lofty heights. Unfortunately, his superb career was under-fired due to injury. He won 24 games in 1952 to cop the American League MVP. He won eight Gold Gloves. He was a three-time All Star. In his MVP season, he dominated the stats. Shantz led his circuit in wins, winning percentage and strikeout-to-walk ratio. He issued the fewest walks per nine innings. He ranked second in complete games. He ranked third in strikeouts, ERA, and shutouts. He seemed poised for many more great years. However, in the latter stages of the '52 campaign, he was plunked by Senators' chucker Walt Masterson.

"I loved to hit," laughs Shantz. "I was determined to get a hit on that particular pitch. I was stepping into the pitch, and by the time I saw it, it was coming at my head. It was too late to get out of the way. I threw my hand up and boom! For years Connie Mack tried to talk me out of batting right-handed. He told me I should protect my left arm and not expose it to the pitch. Turns out he was right. I didn't know anything was wrong with my hand until I got back out to the mound and picked up the ball. Then I was in pain.

"You know, the major leaguers hold 44 golf tourneys a year. I usually go to the one in Washington. I've run into Walt Masterson several times there over the years. We still joke about that HBP. Walt always asks, 'Why the hell didn't you get out of the way?'"

After winning 18 in '51 and 24 in '52, Bobby's statistics plummeted because of the injury. He could not manage more than five wins in any single season from '53 through '56. In '57 as a Yankee, however, he staged a remarkable comeback. He won 11 and earned another berth on the All-Star squad. After that, he changed his style, morphing into a crafty pitcher who threw a variety of pitches. He posted sterling statistics from then on until he called it quits after '64.

SETTING THE STAGE

Bobby Shantz didn't know it at the time but on June 15, 1964, he became an unwitting principle in one of baseball's more famous/infamous trades (one that ranked up—or is that "down?"— with the Phillies' trading Ryne Sandberg away to the Cubs or—forgive me LA—the Larry Andersen for Jeff Bagwell trade). The Cardinals dealt Shantz along with Ernie Broglio and Doug Clemens to the Chicago Cubs for Lou Brock, Jack Spring, and Paul Toth. Lou Brock, of course, went on to be a Hall of Famer.

On August 15 of that same year, the Phillies were looking for some short (no pun intended) relief help. They purchased Shantz in what turned out to be a wise move.

Along with Jack Baldschun, Shantz was a vital cog in the Phillies bullpen down the stretch. When Bobby arrived on August 15, the Phillies enjoyed a four-game lead over the San Francisco Giants. They built that lead up to six games by September 17. That's the day the Phillies took the field to start a crucial four-game series in Los Angeles against the Dodgers. Bobby had been used exclusively in short relief until that point. By season's end, he had pitched only 32 innings, but his best innings were the 7 ⅔ he turned in on September 17. Unexpectedly, he ended up locking horns with one of the Dodger aces, Don Drysdale, and Shantz came out on top.

THE GAME OF MY LIFE
SEPTEMBER 17, 1964
BY BOBBY SHANTZ

I never expected to stay in there for so many innings that day (7⅔). It was just one of those things. Rick Wise was the starter and he injured himself after about four batters. Rick was only 19 at the time. People don't realize what great poise he had for such a young guy in the middle of a pennant race. But this day he got hurt and had to exit. Mauch put me in. Mauch just told me to go as long as I could. Fortunately we had a big first inning.

Tony Gonzalez was our leadoff batter. He started things off with a single. It seemed like every time you turned around that year, Tony was on base. We scored three that inning and took the quick lead we were looking for. If you didn't get to Drysdale early, you were in for a long day. Then Rick went out to the mound and I think their first four guys got on base. All of a sudden the score was 3–2 with only one out and a couple of Dodgers on base. Wise was hurt and that's when I was inserted. I struck out two guys and got out of the inning, but we knew we were in for a tough game with Drysdale on the hill. The Dodgers' two runs gave him new life. Just as we expected, he got tougher as the game wore on. I went through a few innings—how many innings was it? (Answer: the second through the fourth)—where I set them down 1-2-3.

I have myself to blame for coming out of that good rhythm. I tried to bunt in the top of the sixth and popped out into a double play. I always prided myself on my hitting. I could handle the bat and I was normally a decent bunter, but I bunted us right out of the inning that time. The next inning, the Dodgers tied the game with a run. Ironically, they got that run on a couple of bunts. Maury Wills opened the Dodgers' sixth with a bunt single. Wes Parker bunted him to second. Tommy Davis followed with a single to plate Wills for the tie.

Drysdale and I both settled down for a couple of innings. Then in the top of the ninth, Ruben Amaro—a smart player and one of the smoothest glove men I ever saw—took one for the team. Drysdale plunked him and Amaro eventually scored when Dick Allen grounded out. When we took the field, Mauch pulled me out of the game. I know he thought I was tired. I wasn't—but then again, I hadn't pitched that many innings for a long time so I can't really question his decision. The guy slated to lead off (Derrell Griffith) that inning was left-handed so I tried to convince Mauch to keep me in. But he didn't buy it. Jack Baldschun came in and set the Dodgers down one-two-three. I got the win—my only win ever as a Phillie. But it was a big one at the time. Who would have thought what was in store for us over the next week and a half?

WRAPPING IT UP

Two days after Bobby Shantz' masterpiece, the Phillies ended up on the losing end of a debilitating 16-inning loss to the Dodgers. In a painful harbinger of what some historians consider the play that sealed their fate in '64, Willie Davis stole home to steal a victory from the Fightins. A scant two days later, Chico Ruiz reprised that theft, stealing home for a 1-0 Cincinnati victory that kicked off the Phils' disastrous 10-game losing streak.

However, that Phillies-Dodgers, five-hour, 13-minute, 16-inning marathon drained the Phillies. Following a truncated night of sleep after the extra-inning affair, Philadelphia played the getaway game the next day. Philadelphia won behind Jim Bunning. Immediately after the victory, the team winged its way back to Philly. The following day, their season—and the soul of their city—fell apart.

Shantz made his final Phillie (and major-league) appearance on September 29, 1964—three days after his fortieth birthday. He was the third oldest National Leaguer that year. Shantz called it quits despite a glittery 1964 2.25 ERA as a Phillie.

"Mauch asked me to come back," Shantz recalls. "But I had pitched in so much pain for my last five years. I had taken so much cortisone. I didn't want to risk taking any more. The doctors scared me. They said if I continued, I could injure myself and suffer the rest of my life. That was enough for me. I called it quits. I felt blessed to have been a Phillie before I quit. It was a thrill to spend my last year here in Philly. And when I look back, they were simply wonderful years. I wouldn't trade them for anything."

CHAPTER 28

JOHN VUKOVICH

"I didn't exactly have what you'd call a Hall of Fame playing career," John Vukovich told me prior to his death in early 2007. "But I was beaten out for the third-base job twice by Hall of Famers. Well, one of them isn't in the Hall of Fame. He just should be. How many third basemen can you name that ever played this game, who would have started ahead of Mike Schmidt or Pete Rose? I did have one game that I'll always remember. I didn't even start the game. I substituted for another guy who should be a Hall of Famer—that would be Dick Allen. Then I filled in for a Hall of Famer, Mike Schmidt, and hit a homer off a pitcher who probably should be in the Hall of Fame. Now I was no great shakes of a ballplayer, but that's a hell of a day for anyone."

MEET JOHN VUKOVICH

John Christopher Vukovich was born in Sacramento, California. He insisted he was born to make a life out of baseball.

"I was always a decent fielder," he asserted.

He was the district fielding leader throughout his high school career at Amador County High in Sutter Creek, California. After the Phillies tagged him as their number-one choice in the '67 draft, he began a five-year minor-league career before getting his shot at the majors. He starred on a '67 Spartanburg squad that took the Sally League championship. He went on to Reading, where in '69 he led Eastern League third-sackers in fielding. Vukovich wasn't a bad hitter in the minor leagues. In 1970, he socked 22 home runs, drove in 96 runs, and hit .275. Those figures earned him a trip to the Big Show. Naturally, he also led all Pacific Coast League glovemen at his position with a .954 fielding percentage.

Vukovich was called up by the Phillies late in September of 1970 and went 1-for-8 in three games. Thanks to that call-up, Vuke became one of the rare breed that appeared in a Phillies uniform in Connie Mack Stadium, the Vet, and Citizen's Bank Park.

The season following his September call-up, he won the starting third-base position. Vukovich did not exactly nestle into a pantheon of memorable Phillie third basemen (like Pinky Whitney, Puddin' Head Jones, Dick Allen, etc.). He hit a measly .166 with no home runs in 74 games. His defense in contrast was unassailable. In fact, he outdid the National League's third-base Gold Glove recipient, the Astros' Doug Rader in fielding average.

Nonetheless, at the season's end he found himself on the trading block. In a seven-player blockbuster deal with the Milwaukee Brewers, the Phillies gave up not only Vukovich but also fellow third baseman Don Money. In one fell swoop the Phillies had emptied their third-base reserves and bet it all on a rookie named Mike Schmidt.

Vuke's "Brew Crew" years proved to be his pinnacle as a hitter. In two seasons in Milwaukee, although he averaged a strikeout every four at-bats, Vuke showed some pop. He hit five of his six career home runs while playing for Milwaukee. They came off an esteemed group, too: Nolan Ryan, Mickey Lolich, and Sparky Lyle. In 1974, his career year, he slammed three homers, knocked in 11, and posted a .313 slugging percentage in 80 plate appearances.

He was dealt to Cincinnati in '75. Sparky Anderson figured he needed more punch in the offense than Vukovich could supply, so Anderson converted Pete Rose from an outfielder to a third baseman. Rose's departure from the outfield freed a slot for Ken Griffey Sr. to start. Vukovich filled his role as backup and defensive replacement admirably as the "Big Red Machine" won the World Series that year.

He returned to the Quaker City in 1976 in time for the most sustained period of excellence in the Phillies' history. Vukovich clung to a roster slot for the next five years, yet never made more than 62 plate

John Vukovich is one of the few Phillies who has appeared at Connie Mack Stadium, Veterans Stadium, and Citizens Bank Park. *Photo by Brace Photography*

appearances in any single year. In fact, in three of those five years, his plate appearances could be measured in single digits.

Vukovich hung up his spikes after the '81 season and launched a long coaching career with the Chicago Cubs in 1982. He served as first base, third base, and bench coach until the 1987 season. At that point, he hooked on with the Phillies as a coach. He kept that gig for the next 17 seasons. He worked under six different Phillies managers and fulfilled virtually the same role with the Phillies as he had with the Cubs. His other duties included coordinating spring training and working with the team's infielders. In 1994, Vuke made his only All-Star appearance when he coached on the National League All-Star squad.

Vukovich was known as a crusty throwback—opinionated and single minded. An old crony, who insisted on remaining anonymous, says, "Vuke was often wrong but never in doubt."

Though his straightforward style put some people off, he gained the respect of most of his peers and made numerous friends in the game.

"Vuke always reviewed the hitters with me before I was scheduled to start a game," says Curt Schilling, who remembers Vuke's wry sense of humor. "He wanted me to throw Jason Kendall curve balls. So I threw Kendall a curve ball in his first at-bat. Kendall hit a home run. I was just waiting to hear what Vuke would say when I got back to the dugout. Vuke said, 'I didn't tell you to throw a hanging curve ball.' "

In 2004, his final season in the coaches box, he became the longest tenured coach in Phillies franchise history, surpassing the mark of former bullpen coach Mike Ryan.

In 2000, Vukovich served as a coach for the MLB All-Star team that traveled to Japan and in 2004 he was named the recipient of the first Dallas Green Special Achievement Award, presented by the Philadelphia chapter of the Baseball Writers Association of America. The Award recognized Vuke's longevity with the Phillies as a coach.

When he called it quits as a coach, he moved into the general office, serving as special assistant to the general manager, working under Ed Wade and Pat Gillick.

Vukovich passed away on March 8, 2007, after a battle with brain cancer. In his honor, the Phils wore a black armband throughout the 2007 season.

SETTING THE STAGE

In 1976, the Phils were in the thick of things for the first time in years. They had shown much promise the season before, finishing the '75 campaign in second place. Three of their starters—Dave Cash, Larry Bowa, and Greg Luzinski—along with pitcher Tug McGraw had been selected to the '75 All-Star team (Mike Schmidt, despite his league-leading 38 round-trippers, was overlooked). Fueled by Cash's "Yes We Can" sloganeering, the Phillies '76 edition was cleaning up the competition on its way to 101 wins. The '76 All-Star spectacle was staged at the Vet. It was a Philly showcase—a franchise-best five Phils made the squad.

When the final series of the season rolled around, the Phils were safely ensconced in first place. The Mets were in town to finish up the season. The Phillies under skipper Danny Ozark were cautious about losing momentum before entering the team's first postseason fray in decades. The three-game Mets series opened on Friday, October 1 at Veterans Stadium. The always-tough Jerry Koosman, who had already won 21 games that season, was on the hill for New York.

THE GAME OF MY LIFE
OCTOBER 1, 1976
BY JOHN VUKOVICH

I didn't start that day. What else is new, right? We were going up against Koosman, who was always tough on us. I guess he was tough on everyone. Even though we had the division locked up, we were still looking to win. There's no use going out on the field if you're not going out there to win.

We had Tommy Underwood on the hill. Tommy could be tough when he had his control. He didn't overpower you, but when he was hitting his spots, he could tie guys up. He happened to be 'on' that day and he gave us a quality start. They didn't call them quality starts in those days, but that's what it was. He held the Mets to a run in six innings. Then we brought Ron Reed and Gene Garber in. That was the script all year. Those guys—that bullpen—got us a lot of wins.

In this game, during our half of the first we touched up Koosman for a run. We were hoping he didn't have his good stuff that day—but he did. And a guy like Koosman pitches himself into the game, which is just what Koos did. After the first inning, he shut us down. Runs got tough to come by.

Somewhere around the middle of the game, the Mets strung a few hits together and got a run off Underwood. We had ourselves a tie game. I came in the next inning replacing Dick Allen at first base. I came up to the plate in the seventh and hit a shot down third base. Their third baseman—it was some kid they had brought up—muffed it and I got on base. That was the first time I had reached base all season! Then Boonie (Bob Boone) grounded into a double play and I was off the basepaths as fast as I got there. One batter later and we were out of the inning.

In the eighth, Schmidty struck out and Ozark pulled him to give him a rest. I switched positions from first base to third base. In the ninth, Garber set the Mets down one-two-three so I ended up getting an at-bat in the ninth. Well, I got lucky. Koosman got one up and in. Maybe he was tiring or maybe he wanted to get the season over with. Nah, not Koosman! He was too much of a gamer. I saw this pitch real good. I turned on it, got all of it, and it went out. What do you think of that? I hit a walk-off homer off Jerry Koosman! I don't care whether you're Mike Schmidt or John Vukovich, that's a hell of a thrill.

WRAPPING IT UP

The Phils went on to sweep the Mets series. The next day, Jim Lonborg took the hill against Jon Matlack and the Phils walked away with a 7–4 win. In the season finale, Steve Carlton bested the New Yorkers 2–1, which seemed to bode well for the playoffs. Unfortunately, it didn't. The Big Red Machine—the team Vuke had helped the season before—swept the Phils 3–0. The Phils had to struggle through another three seasons before they finally grabbed the brass ring.

CHAPTER 29

RICO BROGNA

"I had so many great games here," says Rico Brogna. "Philly is a terrific place for a ballplayer. It's a terrific place to live. My wife and young daughter loved the city. My son wasn't born yet when I was a Phillie. Philadelphia has a small-town feel. I can't explain it. It's like you're playing for the fans there personally—like playing for a small-town team. Yet, at the same time, Philadelphia is a big city with big-city things to do and see. So it's the fans, the people of Philadelphia that make so many games memorable.

"One game I could easily choose as the 'Game of My Life' is the game that I made my first appearance after coming back from an injury," remembers Brogna. "At that point, it was obvious I wasn't going to be part of the Phils' plans going forward. They had already obtained Travis Lee. But in this particular game, I was in the on-deck circle ready to pinch hit for the first time since I was injured. When they announced my name, I got an ovation that made my eyes tear. What a feeling. All those people on their feet at once—I'll never forget that moment.

"But there were other games that had more excitement—games that were more important to the team," he says. "And when you asked me to think about my answer a few days ago, I think the game that popped into my mind the most was a game against the Braves in 1998. It was a coming-of-age game for our team. We had finished last place the year before. The Braves dominated the division and we finished far behind, but I think we gained a lot of respect that year despite a mediocre record. In this particular game, I had a good game personally. But what made it most memorable was the way we battled back from behind. That became a trademark of our team for the rest of the year."

MEET RICO BROGNA

Rico Joseph Brogna was born in Turners Falls, Massachusetts, where his family remained until he was about seven. At that point, the Brognas headed to Connecticut where Rico became a star baseball and football player. On June 1, 1988, he was drafted by the Detroit Tigers in the first round (26th pick overall) of the 1988 amateur draft. He was signed on June 18, 1988. He got his first chance to perform for the parent club four years later. He started his major league career off hot, batting .364 after his first three starts for the Tigers. One of those hits was his first major league homer. However, he tailed off after that. He was batting only .192 on August 19 when he made his last appearance for the Tigers.

He languished in the minors the entire '93 season before being traded to the Mets in '94 for Alan Zintner. Brogna responded with a superb rookie season in the Big Apple. In 131 plate appearances, he hit a brisk .351. The following year he was the Mets' regular first baseman. He batted .289 and slammed 20 homers. Those numbers and his slick play at the first sack caught the Phillies' attention. Consequently, on November 27, 1996, the Phillies traded Toby Borland and Ricardo Jordan for Brogna.

He became a solid contributor to the Phillies attack for the next three years. He led the team in games played in 1999 and knocked in over a hundred runs in both '98 and '99. His 102 RBIs in '98 were tops on the team. Although he was no gazelle, he was an alert ballplayer, and in '97, he managed to swipe 12 bases in 15 attempts, which was the best stolen-base percentage on the team.

Over the course of his Phillies years, a physical condition that had been identified years earlier plagued Rico more and more, ultimately denying him from realizing his full potential. His condition was diagnosed when he was just 21 after he had only three years of professional baseball under his belt. At the time, he had been experiencing stiffness in his back and hips. He was informed that he had a disease known as ankylosing spondylitis—an inflammatory arthritis of the

The popular Rico Brogna knocked in over 100 RBIs twice as a Phillie. *David Seelig/Getty Images*

spine and pelvic joints. The disease is a chronic, painful, progressive inflammatory arthritis that affects primarily the spine and sacroiliac joints and eventually causes fusion of the spine. Suffice it to say, his career—and the success he enjoyed in spite of this painful ailment—bears testimony to his courage.

"The disease had an impact every day I played," Brogna confirms. "It caused me to suffer severe aches and pains. But I tried to make the best of it. The condition forced me to take better care of myself. I learned to eat right and made sure I got my proper rest. I had to train extra hard just to stay loose. Before each game, I religiously followed a demanding routine. I would take a warm whirlpool and do lots of stretching exercises to get loose. Whereas other guys only needed a half-hour to prepare for a game, it took me hours. Same thing after the game—I needed to cool down in a tub of ice because my joints got so inflamed.

In 2000, He was plagued with injuries and was struck from the regular roster. On July 26, the Phillies traded for first baseman Travis Lee, who came to Philadelphia via the Diamondbacks who anteed up Lee, Omar Daal, Nelson Figueroa, and Vicente Padilla for Phillies' staff ace, Curt Schilling.

"I knew my days as a Phil were numbered once we got Travis," Brogna admits.

The Phillies wasted little time putting Brogna on waivers. On August 3, 2000, the Red Sox picked him up. Less than two weeks later, Brogna enjoyed his greatest moment as a Bostonian. In a tie game against the Devil Rays, he went in as a pinch runner for Brian Daubach and stayed in the game. The following inning, with the bases loaded and two out, he unloaded on a Billy Taylor pitch and slammed a walk-off grand slam. His Beantown stint proved more disappointing than successful, however. At season's end, the Sox granted him free agency. Atlanta picked him up on December 13 and Brogna headed south for what proved to be his final year as an active player. He batted only 203 times for Atlanta. His home-run production tumbled to three and he called it quits before season's end.

"My family and I wanted some finality to our plans for the future," Brogna suggests. "I started the season off in good shape. Then physically I began to deteriorate. I had been platooning with Wes Helms all season. But once the Braves signed Ken Caminiti, he started every game and we sat. There were other signals that I didn't fit into the Braves' plans. They stopped inserting me in situations where they had called on me in the past. All those things played into my decision to retire. I quit and opened up a roster position for Bernard Gilkey. After I quit, other teams called me. I admit I considered some of the offers, but I decided it was better to call it quits."

After retirement, Brogna coached high school football at Kennedy High School in Waterbury. For a number of years, he had been an assistant football coach during baseball's off-seasons. He was now poised to start climbing the football coaching ranks.

"I was prepared to accept a coaching position at a Division III college," he reveals. "But the offer to scout came in from the Diamondbacks at the same time. When I was in high school, I was probably more of a football player than a baseball player. As a high school senior, I signed a letter of intent with Clemson. I was a quarterback and I was looking forward to playing down there—but I opted for baseball instead."

These days, he performs his responsibilities as a major league scout while still battling his disease.

"My wife is a rock," Brogna emphasizes. "She's understanding and helpful dealing with the disease and helping me with some tasks that are difficult."

Brogna is also a celebrity spokesperson for the Spondylitis Association of America, and gives talks to raise money for the Arthritis Foundation.

SETTING THE STAGE

In 1997, the Phillies had finished dead last. After 14 years of service, Darren Daulton was no longer with the club. He rejoined '93 mate Jim Eisenreich in Florida where each of them finally earned a championship ring. Brogna, with his outstanding glove work, 20 round-trippers, and 81 RBIs, proved a productive addition to the depleted '97 Phils roster. Scott Rolen knocked in 92 and put 21 over the fence. Curt Schilling went 17–11 with a 2.91 ERA and a league-leading 319 Ks, but the team was lackluster and out of the pennant chase quickly. They limped out of the gate, losing four of their first five and settling into last place.

A month later, the Phillies found themselves 13.5 games behind the pace. Another month later, the Phils were still last and trailing the next-to-last NY Mets by a whopping 21 games. The Phils finished the season a dismal 33 games behind the front-running Braves. Philly fans abhor silence, so in the absence of reasons to cheer the Phillies, E-A-G-L-E chants reverberated season-long throughout the Vet.

Hope springs eternal, as Alexander Pope opined in eighteenth-century London. Had he been a twentieth-century Philadelphian, the Pope-ster might not have been so inspired. After all, one World Series championship in a century-plus of competition is not the stuff of inspiration. Yet every spring, Philadelphians feel like, "This just might be the year."

Thus began the 1998 baseball season—yet another season of hope for Philly. But 1998 started with a bang after some initial sputtering. In what had (and has) become a local rite, the Phillies lost the opener in New York. Curt Schilling tossed eight scoreless innings, surrendering a lone hit and whiffing nine. However, the Phillies went 14 scoreless innings to the Mets' 13. The Mets tallied a run off Ricky Bottallico in their half of the 14th to claim a 1–0 victory. The Phillies squeaked out a 6–5 win the following day before dropping a pair to the Braves. Philly's tsunami of hope was starting to dwindle down to a Shark Island wave. At that point, Schilling chipped in with a 2–1 win, besting Greg Maddux at the peak of the latter's Hall of Fame career (the former's Hall of Fame credentials are "on the bubble," as they say, due to injuries in what would have been Schilling's most productive seasons).

Schilling's win lit a fire.

The Phillies came north to open the Vet season and swept the defending world-champion Marlins. Beating the champs is always uplifting, but the 1998 edition of the Marlins was a mere shadow of the '97 championship squad. The Marlins had staged a veritable fire sale after their 1997 championship. They dumped a constellation of stars like Moises Alou, Bobby Bonilla, Kevin Brown, Gary Sheffield, and Mike Piazza. Connie Mack would have been proud. In any event, Florida would go on to lose 108 games that year and the Phillies series sweep accounted for all but two of those losses.

The sweep upped Philadelphia's record to 4–3—good for a second-place tie with Atlanta. And wouldn't you know it, the Braves were coming to town for a four-game series. Schilling started the series off with a 1–0 masterpiece. At this point in the young campaign, Schilling's ERA was an other-worldly 0.35. The Phillies split the next two games and entered the following game one game behind the Mets, who had usurped the number-one slot as the Braves and Phillies were slugging it out.

"The Phils were starting to come alive again," Brogna recalls. "Phillies teams always love to beat the Braves, and we were getting pumped up because we felt we could beat them."

THE GAME OF MY LIFE
APRIL 13, 1998
BY RICO BROGNA

I remember this game so well because we came from behind and beat Atlanta. They were always the team to beat. Whether the final standings in 1998 showed it or not, we had a never-say-die attitude on our club. We were a bunch of relative unknowns who relished the underdog role. Our team had a blue-collar mentality. That's the way we approached the game. Guys like Scott Rolen, Doug Glanville, Gregg Jeffries, Curt Schilling and Mike Lieberthal played the game hard. The underdog tag spurred us all on and this game in particular captured the spirit of our team.

We fell way back early on in the contest (specifically in the third inning when the Braves strung together a double, HBP, double, and home run to surge ahead 4-0). We answered with a run but the next inning, the Braves scored a bunch more (the Braves added three). Being down 7–1 against the Braves with Denny Neagle on the hill isn't promising (Neagle went on to a 20–5 season and a Cy Young Award). In the fifth inning, Scott Rolen hit a two-run homer, Mike Lieberthal followed with a single and I came up. Neagle made a mistake and I got all of it for a two-run homer. We had a four-run inning and we were right back in the game (Braves 7, Phillies 5).

Our pitchers were holding them at that point in the game. We sent the top of the order up in the seventh—and everybody hit. When I got to the plate, the score was tied and we had just knocked out a guy named Kerry Ligtenberg. The Braves brought a leftie in to face me—a guy named Adam Butler. There were two on, nobody out. Up until then, there was a knock against me that I couldn't hit lefties. I was facing a situation where most managers would have bunted to avoid a double play. While Butler was taking his warm-up pitches, our manager, Terry Franconia, called me over to the dugout.

He said, "Rico, normally I'd bunt but I'd rather not take the bat out of your hands. I want to give you a chance to shoot a double in the gap and break this thing open."

That vote of confidence did a lot for me. I was fortunate to get a pitch I could turn on. I hit a liner deep to right field that cleared the wall. The crowd's reaction was electric. The Vet was rocking. This was the Braves. I really think that hit got the city to believe in us and get behind the team. It seemed we came alive after that hit. We scored a bunch (the inning ended with the Phillies leading 11–7).

It wasn't a *perfect* day for me. Perfect days are few and far between. I struck out my next time up, but we were ahead at that point and our relievers held on. When we left the park that night, we had won the series three games to one. We had come back from a huge deficit to beat one of baseball's best pitchers. And we were in first place for the first time in a long time.

WRAPPING IT UP

Unfortunately, the first-place gig didn't last. The following day, a loss to the Marlins dropped the Phillies out of first. Schilling's first loss of '98 was a 3–2 heartbreaker that "skyrocketed" his ERA up to 1.09—Philadelphia proceeded to lose the next four and tumble to third.

The Phillies hovered around .500 deep into the season. As late as July 29, they were 55–50 and still in the wild-card hunt. Unfortunately, it was mostly downhill after that. The Phillies finished the season ensconced in third place as the Braves ran away with the division title once again.

CHAPTER 30

DOUG GLANVILLE

"A couple of games come to mind," says Doug Glanville. "The first one comes to mind for what, I guess you could call, selfish reasons. The other is the first game after 9/11. That game had a lot of significance for me. I was the first batter and the roar of the crowd and the electric feeling in the ballpark were unforgettable. I got a hit. I didn't get much wood on the ball, but I hit a single and it was a moment I'll never forget.

"You asked me to pick a Phillies game of my life. Well, I had a game I'll never forget when I played for the Cubs in the 2003 NLCS. In game three at Pro Player Stadium, we were tied after nine innings with the Marlins. James Lofton had singled to left and I went in to pinch hit for our pitcher Joe Borowski. Braden Looper came in to pitch to me and I tripled to center. Lofton scored the go-ahead run, which turned out to be the winning run. How could I ever forget that? To drive in the winning run in such a big game is every player's dream.

"As for my career with Philadelphia," he continued. "I suppose the game that I'd pick as the game of my life is the game where I got my 200th hit for the season. I remember that game for a couple of reasons."

MEET DOUG GLANVILLE

Douglas Metunwa Glanville spent most of his early life in Teaneck, New Jersey. His father was an immigrant from Trinidad, and

211

his mother was a math teacher at Teaneck High School. His mother pressed Glanville into service on Saturday mornings tutoring students who needed math help; however, it wasn't his mother or father who served as Glanville's driving wheel in baseball.

"My brother is passionate about baseball," he reveals. "He taught me a lot about passion for this game. He tried out for professional baseball himself until he was 28. He used to misrepresent his age in those later years, but it was his love of the game that motivated me and made me want to succeed."

Doug wound up with a scholarship to Penn (he turned down offers from Princeton, Duke, Yale, and Brown). He was Penn's top player, and spent the summer following his sophomore season playing baseball in the nation's top summer league. He had to square off against some of the best prospects in the nation from some of the nation's top collegiate baseball programs. Glanville proved his mettle. He hit .331, third best in the circuit. He was named the Top Pro Prospect of the summer league. In the summer of his junior year, he hit .414. His performance and accomplishments lent credence to his potential as a top draft choice.

Glanville graduated Penn with a B.S.E. in Systems Science and Engineering from the School of Engineering. He currently serves on the U of P Board. The Chicago Cubs drafted the fleet 6-foot-2, 170-pounder in the first round (12th pick overall) of the 1991 amateur draft. He made his major-league debut at age 25 on June 9, 1996, versus Montreal—not a memorable day because he took the collar in four at-bats. Glanville had only 83 at-bats that season in posting a .241 average. The Cubs outfield of Luis Gonzalez, Sammy Sosa, and Brian McRae was pretty formidable to break into.

The following year (1997), with Luis Gonzalez departed via free agency to Houston, Glanville moved into the left-field starting slot. He responded with a .300 batting average and 19 stolen bases in a full season's work. However, as Doug puts it, "The Cubs gave up on me."

He had speed and natural ability, which perhaps fueled Cub expectations of the young outfielder excessively. Consequently, on December 23, 1997, Glanville became a Phillie in exchange for Mickey Morandini. The Phillies released Midre Cummings, who wound up with the BoSox, that same off-season. Cummings had

Doug Glanville's 204 hits and .324 batting average in 1999 were both career highs. *Jamie Squire/Getty Images*

been the Phillies most frequent starter in centerfield in '97. The centerfield position, Glanville's most natural slot, was there for the taking.

He earned the '98 starting spot for the Phillies and responded with a solid season. He hit .271 with 23 steals, while getting caught only six times. He also fashioned a glittery .995 fielding percentage. In one stretch, he ripped off one of the Phillies' longest batting streaks in history—his 18-game streak ranks 27th highest on the club's all-time list. His 189 hits placed him tenth in the NL in that category. He also ranked eighth in triples and in the great Whitey Ashburn centerfielder tradition, led the Senior Circuit in both singles (146) and putouts (511).

The following season (1999) was his crowning achievement. Glanville hit .325, eighth best in the NL. He slapped out 204 hits—second best in the league. He scored 101 times and chipped in with a career-high 73 RBIs, and also swiped 34 bases and was nabbed only twice.

The next two seasons, his batting average tumbled although he flashed a power surge in 2001. Doug had never before hit more than 11 round-trippers. However, he upped that total to 14 in 2001. Incidentally, Glanville ranks fourth on the Phillies' all-time list for leadoff homers (eight).

He was granted free agency in October 2002 and signed with the Texas Rangers, where he batted .271 in 195 at-bats. On July 30, however, the Rangers traded him back to the Cubs, who were seeking depth and insurance in the midst of a pennant run. Glanville made only 55 plate appearances for Chicago that season and the Cubs granted him free agency shortly after the campaign ended.

In 2004, the Phillies brought him back into the fold. He got only 162 at-bats and had an uncharacteristic .210 batting average. Following the season, he was again granted free agency. After being picked up and released by the Yankees, he decided to call it quits.

"I had to play catch-up in the business world," he confesses. "Being a baseball player, I missed out on that portion of my life experience. But I got together with a guy who's been a friend of mine since high school and we got involved with building homes—green, environmentally friendly homes—in Chicago.

"I do miss the camaraderie of baseball. It's fulfilling to compete at the highest level. It's a day-by-day high. But my dad was sick starting in 2000. He experienced multiple health problems with diabetes, a stroke, and heart problems. He died the final game of the 2002 season. It was quite a strain, and it took its toll on me.

"When the Yanks released me in 2005, I thought it was a little strange. They had been having problems in centerfield and I think I could have helped. I had a chance to go to San Diego, but it would have involved going to the minors for a spell. I decided against the whole thing. I loved my baseball career, but I was ready to move on."

Glanville got married since he hung up the spikes and hung out his business shingle. In his current role of married businessman, he intends to bring the same commitment to community service he made during his baseball career. As a player, he served as team chairman of the Prostate Awareness Program for Prostate Awareness Day in Major League Baseball. He served on the executive subcommittee of the Major League Baseball Players Association and the Player's Trust for Children. He has worked with the Boys & Girls Club of America, sponsored the American Diabetes Association for the Philadelphia Phillies, and was a founding member of the annual charity drive for the Philadelphia Futures Mentoring Program.

Since his father's death, Glanville helped form the 'Cecil E. Glanville Scholarship Fund' in Teaneck, New Jersey, in honor of his dad. He is a guest writer on many sports websites, including ESPN.com, mlb.com, and yoursportsfan.com.

SETTING THE STAGE

The Phillies were at the tail end of a second consecutive third-place finish under manager Terry Francona as the 1999 campaign wound down. Going into the September 29 contest with the Cubs, neither the Phillies nor the Cubs could look forward to anything other than finishing out another season. The Phillies were 26 games behind the front-running Atlanta Braves, while the hapless Cubs trailed the division-leading Reds by 29½ games. The Phils did manage some bright individual performances that year. Although Larry Walker was running away with the batting title, Bobby Abreu was running neck to neck with Luis Gonzalez for runner-up. Meanwhile, Glanville was running neck to neck for the coveted title of most hits. Glanville went into this game with 199 hits. A crowd of 21,142 showed up at Veterans Stadium to watch the action.

THE GAME OF MY LIFE
SEPTEMBER 29, 1999
BY DOUG GLANVILLE

This game was a personal fulfillment. I felt the Cubs had given up on me prematurely when they traded me. I got tremendous satisfaction out of the fact that I achieved the 200th-hit milestone against the Cubs. Carlton Lower was on the hill for us and we were going up against Micah Bowie.

The Cubs didn't score in the visitor's half of the first. I led off for us with a deep fly to right. I hit the ball well, but the right-fielder caught up to it. I came to the plate again in the third and I hit another fly ball that was caught. We scored that inning and took a 1-0 lead. Then in the fourth, the Cubs had all kinds of troubles. There was a balk, a wild pitch, and a passed ball, and we scored another run. When I got up to the plate, there were two men on. I got a good pitch to drive and I hit it well for a three-run homer. That was a huge thrill. For that to be my 200th hit and to hit it in front of the home crowd against the team that had traded me was fulfilling.

The game stayed pretty much the same: 5–0. I made another out in my next plate appearance. Then in the eighth I singled again (off Rick Aguilera) but I didn't score. That's pretty much how the game ended. We won 5–0. I had two hits and three RBIs. I couldn't have scripted it better.

WRAPPING IT UP

Glanville went on to collect 204 hits that season. His total fell two short of Gonzalez' league-leading 206 safeties. Likewise, Gonzalez edged out Abreu for second place in the batting title. The Phillies finished third in their division. The following year, they tumbled to fifth, and Francona was headed for Beantown and a major exorcism.

CHAPTER 31

CURT SIMMONS

"That's a tough question when you play as long as I did," says Curt Simmons when asked for the game of his life. "It's even tougher when you played as *long ago* as I did. Let's see—what games do I remember? You know, I stole home in 1963. What pitcher wouldn't remember that?"

Simmons—no gazelle was he—had only two stolen bases in 20 years. However, on September 1, 1963, Simmons stole home against the Phillies with Chris Short on the mound and Bob Oldis catching. The Cards and Simmons won 7–3.

"That was a great game," continues Simmons. "Of course, there were so many great games in 1950. That was the most enjoyable season. We were all young and eager, but I suppose the game that sticks out most is my 'almost perfect' game against the Braves."

MEET CURT SIMMONS

Curtis Thomas Simmons was one of the most sought after young ballplayers in the country in the mid- to late forties. He was one of the original "Bonus Babies" as these young recruits were called in that long-ago era. The Carpenter family had purchased the Phillies in the forties and actively tried to resurrect the franchise. However, the Phillies didn't have much of a legacy to resurrect. They had been a perennial doormat since Philadelphia unwisely sent Grover Cleveland Alexander to the Cubs in 1918. From 1919 to 1945, the Phillies—or

Blue Jays as they were sporadically and erratically called in 1943 and '44—finished next to last in 23 of 27 seasons.

Nonetheless, in the mid-forties the Carpenters came to town and started dishing out money to young "phenoms," signing up the heart of what was soon to become the Whiz Kids. The Phillies inked Simmons, Robin Roberts, Del Ennis (Ennis was signed right out of Olney High School in Philly), Richie Ashburn, Dick Sisler, Granny Hamner, Willie Jones, and others. The signings started to pay dividends right away. Ennis won the Major League Rookie of the Year Award in 1946, and Ashburn copped the same award two years later. The Phillies managed to climb out of the basement in the late forties and when Eddie Sawyer took the helm in 1949, they claimed third place, their highest finish since 1917.

Then came 1950, the beginning and end of the city's beloved Whiz Kids, who helped nudge the Philadelphia A's to Kansas City— (but that's a story for another day). These particular turn-of-the-decade days were great ones for Philly sport. The Philadelphia Eagles were the reigning kings of the NFL and the Phillies were the surprise of the baseball world.

"I still think my best season was 1950," Simmons confesses. "I was playing really well and then I got called away for service. I ended up missing the end of the season and the World Series."

He was called to duty for the Korean War. On October 3, 1950, the ruling came down that Simmons, even though he was on Army furlough, was ineligible to play in the World Series. That ruling virtually sank the upstart Whiz Kids who were going up against the powerful Yankees in the midst of one of their most fabled dynasties. Beginning in 1949, the Yankees won the World Series for six straight years. In the decade of the fifties, the Yanks failed to appear in the World Series only two times.

The Phillies boasted three of baseball's top hurlers in 1950: Curt Simmons, 20-game winner Robin Roberts, and Jim Konstanty, who won the NL MVP, NL Pitcher of the Year, and UPI's NL Player of the Year. Good pitching, the argument goes, is the key element in a short series—so who knows? Unarguably, Simmons' absence was detrimental to the team's chances.

Curt Simmons missed a perfect game once because of a lead-off single on his first pitch. *Photo by Brace Photography*

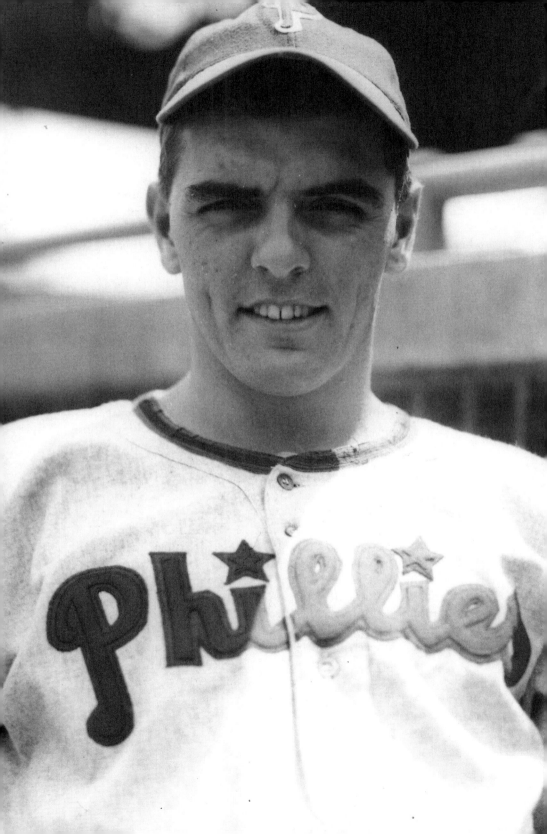

Simmons missed the entire '51 season because of his military duty. He returned in '52 with a 14–8 season that was truncated because of arm trouble. However, he still managed to lead the Senior Circuit in shutouts with six. In fact, Simmons finished in the top ten in shutouts five times in the fifties and three times in the sixties.

In 1953, he was going great guns until he cut his toe in a lawn-mowing accident. In '54, despite a glittery 2.81 ERA, he suffered his first losing season, posting a 14–15 won-lost log. In the next few seasons he remained a mainstay of the Phillies pitching staff until 1958 when he slumped to a 7–14 record and his ERA bloated to 4.38. An elbow operation kept him out for virtually the entire 1959 season.

"I was released in San Francisco at midnight," Simmons reveals about the unceremonious end to his Phillies career in 1960. "I was upset when I left Philly. I don't think they went about releasing me the right way. I was coming off an elbow operation and they got rid of me. The way the club handled my departure wasn't pleasant. It wasn't the way to find out I was leaving a city and team I had played for over the previous 12 years."

Simmons went on to some great seasons in St. Louis. He won seven games for the Cardinals and posted the NL's sixth-lowest ERA in 1960—the year he was dumped by the Phillies. His best season came a few years down the road in '64. He was instrumental in the Cardinals winning the World Series that year.

"I think I had my steadiest season with St. Louis in '64," he says. "I had better stuff when I was younger, but I was much steadier at that point in my career. Those 18 wins were the most I ever had in a season. I also had a good World Series. Just being there was a thrill. I didn't get to face the Yankees in 1950, but I met up with them 14 years later and this time my team won. I went eight innings in a scoreless tie against Jim Bouton. Then Mickey Mantle hit a homer off Barney Schultz who relieved me."

Simmons' performance declined after 1964. He wrapped up his sterling career that spanned 20 seasons in California. He debuted in 1947 as the youngest player in the NL and retired in 1967 as the tenth oldest player in the expanded AL. He was a three-time All-Star.

"Since then, I've been mostly involved with the golf course," Simmons explains. "I don't play as much golf these days though. I had my right hip replaced in September. I've had my left hip replaced twice. My wife has been having health problems over the past few years, so I'm busy taking care of her. I'm kind of the chauffeur-butler these days. But all in all, things are going well."

SETTING THE STAGE

As the 1953 season commenced, there was still a deep well of hope and belief in the Whiz Kids. Roberts, Simmons, Stan Lopata, Ashburn, Ennis, Hamner, and Willie Jones still anchored a very solid team.

The Phillies got out of the gate quickly in '53. Unfortunately, they fizzled as the season wore on. They lost the April 14 opener at home (that's almost a given). Robin Roberts started (that's another given in the fifties). Simmons put a Phillies win on the board the following day. After another loss, the Phillies rolled up eight straight wins which put them atop the NL standings by 2 ½ games on April 28. By May 10, when the Phillies left Brooklyn, after dropping a 13–7 game to Billy Loes, they did some grueling traveling. They played a single game in St. Louis followed by a single game against the Cubs on May 15. They won both. Then they took a train up to Milwaukee for a showdown. The Phils and Braves were tied for first.

The Braves were riding a six-game winning streak going into the May 16 contest with Philadelphia. They boasted a fearsome assembly of right-handed power hitters like Joe Adcock, Del Crandall, Andy Pafko, and Sid Gordon. They also had a promising 21-year-old, left-handed hitting, sophomore sensation named Eddie Matthews, whose mug graced the first-ever edition of *Sports Illustrated*. He was launching prodigious shots out of parks en route to a 47-home run season. Matthews' total set the mark for third-sackers until Mike Schmidt eclipsed it years later.

THE GAME OF MY LIFE
MAY 16, 1953
BY CURT SIMMONS

This was Milwaukee's first year as a big-league city. The Braves had moved there from Boston. One thing I remember so well that day was that every time a Brave hit a ball in the air, the crowd went nuts. Under threatening skies, 23,578 spectators showed up—boosting Milwaukee's ten-game total attendance to 220,541. They were so thrilled to have a major-league club for their city.

The game was a pretty sanitary game actually. I don't recall any great plays. I was throwing exceptionally well that day. I remember I had 11 strikeouts.

Billy Bruton hit my very first pitch for a single and that was about it. People forget Billy Bruton, but he was a great centerfielder in an era of great centerfielders. Besides Willie, Mickey, and the Duke, the fifties was the era of Whitey Ashburn, Bill Virdon, and other terrific centerfielders. I believe Bruton was a rookie that year, though he was an older rookie. Many African American ballplayers were coming into the MLB during this era. The following year, another African American, named Henry Aaron—a young 20-year-old—cracked the Milwaukee roster. I didn't know much about Bruton when I faced him—not that it would have helped.

Milwaukee had a young guy, Don Liddle on the mound. Liddle happened to be a 28-year-old rookie too who lasted only four years in the bigs. I think we chased him early (the Phillies knocked Liddle out in the fourth, tagging him for five hits and two runs). Then, the game settled down pretty much. They put Lew Burdette in, and neither team scored through the middle innings.

In the eighth, we got an insurance run—right-fielder, Mel Clarke doubled and scored on Ennis' single. But that was it. I struck out 11 and didn't walk anyone. I think it was my sixth win—I was going good at the time. I wish every game I ever pitched had gone that smoothly.

WRAPPING IT UP

"That game occurred before my lawnmower incident," Simmons adds. "A little later in the season, I cut my toe badly when I was mowing the lawn. I was off for a month—from June 4 to July 4. A lot of people blamed my decline in performance on the lawnmower incident. They said it changed my motion and caused arm trouble. I'm not so sure. Robin Roberts didn't have arm trouble in those days. Robin had that smooth delivery and I was very herky-jerky in my motion. I think that might have caused my arm problems as much as cutting the toe.

"I still have the baseball from my game against Milwaukee," he adds. "Lopata used to fix the balls up for us after a big game. He'd put the date and score and some things that happened in the game, like a recap—he'd put, 'Curt had trouble today, but he battled hard'—something like that. He would draw a picture on the ball too. Stosh was kind of an amateur artist. I've given some of those balls away, but I still have plenty I'm saving for the grandkids."